A Visitor's Guide to
North Wales
and Snowdonia

The Library of

Crosby Hall

Presented by

Mrs. E. G. Rogers

NORTH WALES
AND SNOWDONIA

Visitor's Guides to Britain

This new series of guide books gives, in each volume, the details and facts needed to make the most of a holiday in one of the tourist areas of Britain and Europe. Not only does the text describe the countryside, villages, and towns of each region, but there is also valuable information on where to go and what there is to see. Each book includes, where appropriate, stately homes, gardens and museums to visit, nature trails, archaeological sites, sporting events, steam railways, cycling, walking, sailing, fishing, country parks, useful addresses — everything to make your visit more worthwhile.

Other titles already published or planned include:
Lake District
Peak District
Chilterns
Yorkshire Dales
Cotswolds
Devon
Cornwall
South Wales Coast

A Visitor's Guide To

NORTH WALES
AND SNOWDONIA

Colin Macdonald

MOORLAND PUBLISHING

British Library Cataloguing in Publication Data

Macdonald, Colin
    A visitor's guide to North Wales & Snowdonia
    1. Wales, North—Description and travel—
    Guide-books
    I. Title
    914.29'104857   DA740.N6

For Sheila and Laura

ISBN 0 86190 049 9 (paperback)
ISBN 0 86190 050 2 (hardback)

©Colin Macdonald 1982

Printed in Great Britain by Redwood Burn Ltd,
Trowbridge, Wiltshire for Moorland Publishing
Company Ltd, PO Box 2, 9-11 Station Street,
Ashbourne, Derbyshire, DE6 1DZ, England

Contents

1   North Wales   11
2   Clwyd, The Afon Dee and The Border Areas   18
3   Clwyd — The Coast and Inland   29
4   The Northern Mountains of Gwynedd   42
5   Gwynedd — Blaenau Ffestiniog, Barmouth and Bala   65
6   The Lleyn Peninsula   78
7   Anglesey — The Isle of Mona   94
    The Language   114
    Further Information for Visitors   116
    Index   128

Illustrations

Page
No

8-9 Y Garn and the Ogwen Valley
12 Eagle Tower, Caernarfon Castle
14-15 Cnicht and the Moelwyns
16 Porthmadog
17 Sheep Shearing
21 Plas Newydd
22 Llangollen Station
23 Canoeing in Llangollen
24 Canal Boats
24 Valle Crucis Abbey
25 Highest Waterfall
26 Stone Circle
28 Ruthin
33 Sun Centre, Rhyl
35 Gwyrch Castle
36 The Little Orme
37 The Great Orme
38 Lewis Carroll Memorial
41 Rhuddlan Castle
44 Conwy Castle
45 Conwy Walls
46 Smallest House
47 Caernarfon Castle
49 Crib Goch, Snowdon
51 Snowdon
53 Llyn Peris and Llanberis Pass
53 Llyn Peris
55 Tryfan, Ogwen Valley
56 Old Pack Horse Bridge
57 Waterloo Bridge
58 Swallow Falls
59 Beddgelert
59 Gelert's Grave
60 Bucket Conveyor
61 Aberglaslyn Pass
62-3 Croesor Valley

64 Small Castle
66 Ffestiniog Railway
68 Llyn Mair
69 Harlech Castle
70 Llandanwg Church
72 Maes Artro
73 Roman Steps
75 Tomen-y-Mur
76 Memorial Stone, Llyn Celyn
79 Llyn Dinas
81 Porthmadog
82 Tramway to quarries
83 Slate Mill
84 Retaining Wall of Old Tramway
84 Old Slate Quarry
85 Llyn Gwynant
86 Sailing near Criccieth
86 Lloyd George's Grave
87 Abersoch Moorings
88 St Tudwals Island
89 Bardsey Island
90 Porthdinllaen
91 Tre'r Ceiri, Hillfort
93 Hells Mouth
95 Menai Straits
95 Britannia Bridge
96 Longest Platform Ticket
98 Telford's Tollhouse
99 Bryn-Celli-Ddu burial mound
100 Visitor centre, Llandwyn Island
102 Roman Walls, Caer Gybi
104 South Stack Lighthouse
106 Amlwch Harbour
108 Hut Circle
110 Penmon Priory
111 Puffin Island
112 Beaumaris Castle Moat

Acknowledgements
I am grateful for all the courteous advice and help I received from the Tourist Information Centres that I visited on my travels, and to the staff of the Snowdonia National Park centre who kindly provided me with information and suggestions. I have a patient wife, Sheila, who eventually typed the manuscript.

Picture credits: Photographs on p12, 14-15, 82, 83, 85 are by L. Porter, p8-9, 55 by J. A. Robey. The remainder are by the author

KEY FOR MAPS

n MUSEUM/ART GALLERY/CENTRE

Z WILDLIFE PARK/ZOO SANCTUARY

▲ ARCHAEOLOGICAL SITE

⊞ BUILDING/ COUNTRY PARK GARDENS

n CASTLES

✳ OTHER PLACE OF INTEREST

Note on the Walks Described

The walks in this book are not intended to be a field-by-field guide, but recommendations for the best routes. Many have been chosen so that they avoid the popular and crowded areas, while many are more interesting or give better views than the better known routes. Walkers must be equipped according to the severity of the terrain: a lakeside stroll or woodland walk requires only stout shoes and weather protection. High level mountain walks need proper boots and clothing, map and compass and the ability to use them correctly. The Ordnance Survey 1:50,000 maps, Sheets 114, 115, 116, 123, 124, 125 are recommended. Also the Ordnance Survey 1:25,000 Outdoor Leisure Map *Snowdonia National Park*.
Mountain Rescue: telephone 999 and ask for mountain rescue.

The walks described have been graded so that a suitable route may be chosen at a glance. Walking time is included, as it is often of more relevance, than distance.

H	High level route for fine weather
M	Medium level route
L	Low level route, often recommended when the weather in the mountains is poor
*	Well signposted
**	Easy to follow with the aid of a map
***	Requires careful map reading
****	Recommended for experienced hill walkers only
o	Least interest
oo	
ooo	
oooo	Most interest

Y Garn and the Ogwen Valley

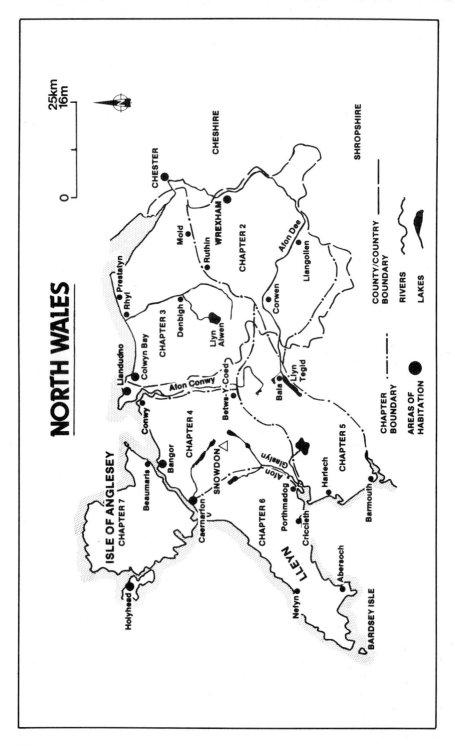

NORTH WALES

ISLE OF ANGLESEY
CHAPTER 7

Holyhead

Beaumaris

Bangor

SNOWDON

Caernarfon

CHAPTER 4

Conwy

Llandudno

Colwyn Bay

CHAPTER 3

Denbigh

Llyn Alwen

Rhyl

Prestatyn

Mold

Ruthin

CHESTER

WREXHAM

CHAPTER 2

Corwen

Afon Dee

Llangollen

CHESHIRE

SHROPSHIRE

Afon Conwy

Betws-Y-Coed

Bala

Llyn Tegid

CHAPTER 5

Afon Glaslyn

CHAPTER 6

Porthmadog

Criccieth

Harlech

Barmouth

Nefyn

LLEYN

Abersoch

BARDSEY ISLE

25km
16m

0

COUNTY/COUNTRY
BOUNDARY — — —

RIVERS

LAKES

CHAPTER
BOUNDARY — · · —

AREAS OF
HABITATION

10

1 North Wales

What is it that makes North Wales so attractive to the visitor and holiday maker? There is probably no single answer, but a combination of many that gives this compact area something of interest and pleasure for everyone. Almost surrounded by golden beaches and blue seas, it is a land of lakes and mountains, of hills and tumbling streams. The spectacular scenery includes some of the highest mountains in Great Britain and a coastline to rival many in Europe.

The further you go into Wales the more obvious it becomes that you are entering another country, particularly as you try to pronounce the tongue-twisting names on the road signs or listen to the lilting accents of a language that is so baffling to both English and Continental visitors. Though spoken throughout the principality it is in the counties furthest from the English border that the Welsh language is spoken the most.

There are many English people living in North Wales, particularly along the north coast, but it is the Welsh people and their language which make the country so different from England. The beautiful scenery and the strange language provide all the ingredients of a holiday abroad without the inconvenience of catching a plane or ferry.

The Welsh people are descended from the early Celtic settlers who came across from Europe in about 400BC. Bringing with them their language and their religion, they cleared the land in the valleys for their first farms and built hilltop village-forts for their refuge and protection.

Their language has remained to form the basis of modern Welsh. Complete extermination by the Romans removed virtually all evidence of the Welsh religious leaders, popularly known as Druids. Their true role in society was that of teacher, judge and administrator as well as religious leader, and it is likely that they live on in spirit in the form of the Eisteddfod. Here the bards (storytellers) meet to compete in poetry or simply to discuss problems; they have filled the gap left when the Romans destroyed the Druids, and are part of Welsh culture.

After the departure of the Romans there were many attempts to subdue the Welsh people. The Irish tried, then the Vikings, then England's Edward I — many occupied the country, but none subjugated it. Though modern Wales must accept that there is little likelihood of devolution and that Government from London must continue, it is a brave man who would say that the struggle is over.

Each of the five counties of North Wales had its own individual character before the local government reorganisation in 1974. But, now that there are only two, Clwyd and Gwynedd, their administration and organisation have become a little more unwieldy, and loyal Welshmen must inevitably wonder if the reorganisation was not another attempt by Westminster to overcome them.

Although there were always differences between the five counties, the two new counties now have little in common. Clwyd, the former counties of Flint and Denbighshire in the north east corner of Wales, is more densely

Eagle Tower, Caernarfon Castle

populated that Gwynedd, and has an industrial belt around Wrexham and on Deeside. On its flat northern coastline — long sandy beaches easily accessible from the industrial north west of England — resorts now cater for both day trippers and longer-stay visitors. Inland, the rounded hills, split by wide, deep valleys, have many places of interest. There are forests, castles, lakes and mansions, and many places for the industrial archaeologist to explore.

Gwynedd, the former counties of Anglesey, Caernarfonshire, Merioneth and a small part of Denbighshire, quieter by comparison, has a coastline of rocky coves and pleasant bays. Welsh is its first language, as the majority of the population have been born and bred in Wales. Of the two counties it has the more dramatic and varied scenery, from the high mountains of Snowdonia to the quiet pastoral lands of the Lleyn Peninsula and Anglesey. Around its coasts the resorts are smaller and less brash than those of Clwyd. Its many castles, beaches and lakes are a constant source of interest and pleasure.

The Snowdonia National Park is in the county of Gwynedd. It is the largest National Park in Wales with an area of 845 square miles. Formed in 1951, it has striven to maintain the balance between visitors and the environment. There are nature reserves, forests, trails and walks, and excellent Tourist Information Offices in many of its towns and villages. Like the other National Parks in Britain most of the land in Snowdonia is in private ownership, — a living and working area where the rights of the farmers and landowners must be respected.

Though named after the highest peak in England and Wales, Snowdon, there is much more to the Park than this actual mountain. The many ranges of hills to the south and west are enough to keep the most ardent climber and rambler happy for years. Stretching 30 miles along the coast of Tremadog Bay and backed by the superb Rhinog Range of hills is a wide sandy beach, also part of the Park; as it is seldom full, and generally warmer than the mountians inland, it is ideal for bathing.

The early economy of North Wales was based upon the varied minerals available for exploitation of the hills. The Romans found lead in the northern limestone hills; they mined copper on Anglesey and gold in the southern parts of Snowdonia. Other miners followed them and found more deposits of copper around Beddgelert and the lakes below Snowdon. North Wales is however best known for its slate industry which flourished in the early nineteenth century:, though now much diminished, it has left plenty of evidence of its extensive workings throughout the hills. Much of the mining took place within the area of the Snowdonia National Park and it is common to come across dangerous open shafts and mine workings during a walk. Common sense should tell you to steer clear of them.

Many old mines, particularly around Blaenau Ffestiniog, are re-opening for visitors, and provide guided tours to the enormous caverns created when the slate was extracted. There are industrial trails around Wrexham, forest trails near Betws-y-Coed and visits to power stations in Snowdonia and Anglesey. The visitor is encouraged to make the most of his surroundings and environment by a people who are fiercely proud of their heritage.

With the mining came narrow gauge railways, that to Ffestiniog being perhaps the most famous. The railway age brought lines throughout Wales, so creating some of the major resorts on the coast, Rhyl, Llandudno, Barmouth and many more. Although the era of the railway in the region has now almost ended, these resorts are still the most popular. There are however many quieter villages on the Lleyn Peninsula and Anglesey untouched by rail.

The last thirty years have seen a dramatic change in leisure activities. Although the railways have declined, the increase in car ownership has made many parts of the country more accessible. Many physical activities have become popular: the hills are ideal for climbers and walkers, the bays and beaches perfect for the yachtsman, while there are many lakes and reservoirs for the fisherman. Around the coast are courses for

Cnicht and the Moelwyns from Glan-y-Gors

golfers and wide estuaries and steep cliffs for ornithologists. The area is so compact that it is not difficult to enjoy a very varied holiday within a short travelling distance.

North Wales, though relatively small, has so much to see and do that any guide book can only touch the surface and give an idea of the many interesting ways of spending one's time. Much of the attraction of Wales is the heritage of its castles, museums, mines and many prehistoric monuments. Around the coast are many tiny ancient churches from the early days of Celtic Christianity and many places associated with early saints; wherever you are, there is always something of interest within a short distance. There is such a variety of activities that it is difficult to give every subject the coverage it requires. Part of the enjoyment of a holiday is exploring and discovering a country or even just a neighbourhood. Many specialist books are available for the enthusiast.

North Wales can be divided easily into separate areas, all with a slightly different character. Clwyd is conveniently divided into the northern coastline and the hills and mountains around Llangollen and Corwen. On the other hand, Gwynedd is so large and varied that it must be divided into four contrasting areas; varying from the lowlands and beaches of Anglesey and the Lleyn Peninsula to the mountains of Snowdonia.

Each area has been considered separately and some ideas have been suggested for visits and walks. These are by no means the only activities available, and a little individual exploration will uncover a wealth of hidden pleasures.

Porthmadog

Sheep Shearing

There are few, if any, properties (either National Trust or privately owned) that are open all year round. As many are open only on summer weekdays, it is always sensible to check visiting hours beforehand with the local Tourist Information Centres.

Some walks are suggested, and while most are fairly easy and can be tackled by the average person, many — particularly within Snowdonia — are more arduous and should not be attempted without due preparation. As the weather can change quickly, extra clothing and waterproofs should always be taken on a long walk. A map, too, adds so much to the enjoy-

ment. A 1:50,000 Ordnance Survey map of the area will be invaluable. Many small areas and forests have their own nature trails or forest trails; individual leaflets are generally available at nearby information offices or shops.

Throughout this guide are suggestions for visits and walks, and at the end of the book is further information for visitors. Every effort has been made to ensure the accuracy of the information and, though space precludes much that may be of interest, it is hoped that visitors will use it as a basis for an enjoyable holiday.

2 Clwyd, The Afon Dee and the Border Area

The River Dee is one of the major rivers of Wales, and it forms a natural boundary to this part of North Wales. It is likely that all visitors to Clwyd will cross it during their journey. From its source at Bala Lake right in the heart of the mountains to the sea near Flint it runs through some of the most beautiful and varied countryside in Wales.

When one enters North Wales from England the scenery changes after crossing the river, and it is not long before one is away from the plains of Cheshire and Shropshire and into the rounded foothills of the Clwydian Range. These hills, formed mainly of hard Silurian rock, run roughly north to south across the county dividing the industrial east from the rural west and give an introduction to the scenery that can be expected as the journey continues.

The eastern foothills which follow the curve of the Dee are composed mainly of coal measures with an underlying bed of limestone that comes to the surface occasionally as the scarp edges south of Maeshafn and on the Eglwyseg Mountains above Llangollen. It was probably the limestone deposits and the minerals in these hills, particularly lead ores, which brought the first industry to the area. It is known that the Romans mined lead here using local labour, but it was not until the sixteenth and seventeenth century, when lead became such an important commodity, that the industry really developed. The most important use for lead was the lining of the roofs of houses and churches. During the heyday of the lead industry money was invested heavily in mining in these limestone hills. The mines stretch from Halkyn Mountain near Prestatyn in the north to Minera west of Wrexham. Massive beam engines were brought up from Cornwall to pump the mines clear of water, but it is only the overgrown square stone remains of the engine houses and their chimneys with the surrounding waste tips which survive as reminders of a once-thriving industry.

Iron ore mined in the hills and coalfields surrounding Wrexham led to the establishment in the eighteenth century of a thriving smelting industry with iron works in Bersham, Ruabon and Wrexham. Other local resources, including clay bricks and tiles, zinc ores and wool from the local sheep, soon made this area the most industrialised and populous in North Wales. Bersham was the main supplier of cannons to the British army during the Peninsular War. The iron ore eventually ran out and the Wrexham-based industry was moved north to a site near Queensferry on the River Dee to allow direct imports of the raw materials by sea. During 1980, however, under Government rationalisation plans for the steel industry, this major employer on Deeside finally closed its doors.

Wrexham and its environs now support a few industries, but most of those based on local resources have declined, leaving their remains only for the industrial archaeologist to explore. This area of Wales is now designated as a development area by the government, and industries large and small are encouraged to move here to provide much-needed employment.

In the centre of Wrexham stands the Church of St Giles, notable for its decorated tower built in 1506 and surmounted by four graceful hexagonal turrets. To the west of the tower is the grave of Elihu Yale, the main benefactor of Yale University in America. It was restored by the members of the university in 1968 to mark the 250th anniversary of this benefaction. A replica of the tower of the church stands at Yale.

About one mile south of Wrexham and standing in a large estate, is the mansion of Erddig Hall, which was started in 1684 and finally completed about 1721-4 by John Meller, a London lawyer. With his nephew Simon Yorke he collected much of the fine silver and gilt furniture that can be seen here today. The property passed to Simon in 1733 and remained in the Yorke family until given to the National Trust in 1973. The family had always been good to their staff and the servants' hall has several portraits of particularly favourite staff. Visitors

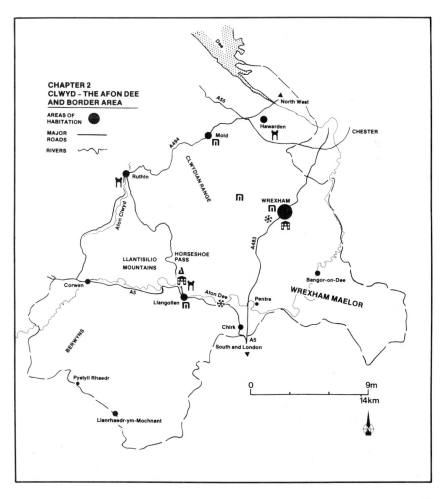

CHAPTER 2
CLWYD – THE AFON DEE
AND BORDER AREA

AREAS OF
HABITATION

MAJOR
ROADS

RIVERS

Places to Visit Near Wrexham

Erddig Hall, off A438, 1 mile south of Wrexham. Seventeenth-century house, beautifully furnished. Outbuildings and workshops showing both sides of life.

St Giles Church, Wrexham near town centre.
Grave of Elihu Yale, fine wrought iron gates and decorated steeple.

Maelor Library and Arts Centre, Rhosddu Road, Wrexham.
Houses visiting exhibitions from national museums.

Bersham Industrial Centre and Trail.
8-mile trail through many points of historical and industrial interest. Leaflet available. Starts at village green on B5426

Geological Museum of North Wales.
On A525 Wrexham-Ruthin road at Bwlch-gwyn.
Displays illustrating geology of North Wales, and colliery machinery and Dinosaur Park.

now enter through the stables and laundry, which, along with the restored sawmill, smithy and bakehouse, give a good idea of the domestic arrangements of an eighteenth-century house.

To the east of Wrexham is an area known as Wrexham Maelor, which projects into the plains of Cheshire and Shropshire. The district was originally known as Maelor Saesneg (Saxon Maelor) and was established by Edward I as a detached part of Flint. Its character is more English than Welsh, as are many of the village names, but it has firmly remained part of Wales through the centuries, despite its vulnerable position. It finally lost its identity, and became part of Clwyd in the early 1970s.

Despite being the most industrial and extensively populated area of North Wales this corner of Clwyd has remained only a narrow strip. The nearby countryside is always accessible and only a short journey is necessary to leave all behind and reach the hills and valleys around Llangollen.

Here is a town so typically Welsh from its greystone houses to its wooded hillsides that it is hard to believe that one is only a few miles from the English border. One needs go no further than Llangollen to experience much of what Wales has to offer, and it has justifiably been a popular tourist centre for many years. George Borrow started his epic Welsh journey here in 1854 by describing Llangollen in his book *Wild Wales* as 'a small town or large village'. The town sits on both sides of the River Dee: the centre, with shops, cafes and hotels on the south bank of the river, is connected by a stone bridge to the thin strip of houses squeezed between the canal and the main road on the north of the river. The bridge was built originally in 1345, but it has been strengthened and improved through the centuries to cope with the increasing volume of traffic which frequently causes quite a bottleneck on a sunny summer's day.

The town is perhaps best known for the International Musical Eisteddfod which is held to the east of the town in July every year. It attracts singers, musicians and dancers from all over the world. The town comes alive with national costumes and a true spirit of international friendship during these weeks.

Plas Newydd, home of the Two Ladies of Llangollen

Half a mile from the town centre is the old house of Plas Newydd, once the house of two eccentric old ladies known throughout the country as the 'Ladies of Llangollen'. The ladies, the Hon Miss Sarah Ponsonby and Lady Eleanor Butler, resided at the house from 1779 until their deaths in 1829 and 1831. They were known for their rather eccentric style of dress and for the variety of their visitors — Wellington, Sir Walter Scott, who later immortalised the house in *The Betrothed*, and Wordsworth, all of whom were expected to contribute to the ladies' collection of old oak curios. Wordsworth's contribution was a rather disdainful sonnet, which was not liked by the ladies — he was not invited back.

There is not much room between the river and the steeply rising hills to the north, but in that short space is squeezed a railway station, now home of the Llangollen Railway Society, a busy main road and a canal. In this limited area it is possible to study transport through the ages, for just above the station is the Canal Exhibition Centre on a spur of the Shropshire Union Canal.

Climbing steeply from just opposte the canal bridge is a footpath to Castell Dinas Bran, a stone castle perched 1,000ft above the town. Originally the site of an Iron Age hillfort, it later became a Norman castle and, finally, a little used stone castle built in 1236 which had become a ruin by 1578. The climber is rewarded by a fine view — the long limestone escarpment of Eglwyseg Rocks and the valleys radiating to the west and the north of the town. It is a magnificent place for a castle.

A narrow road rises steeply from the bridge and runs up the valley below Eglwyseg Mountain to the ford at World's End. There is parking space below the ford and a short walk

Llangollen Station (home of the Llangollen Railway Society) and the River Dee

Places to Visit Near Llangollen

Pontcysyllte Aqueduct
Carries canal 120ft above River Dee, 1,000ft long. Superb position.

Plas Newydd
House of Ladies of Llangollen, beautiful black and white house in lovely gardens. South of river, well signposted.

Castell Dinas Bran
Thirteenth-century hilltop castle. Dominates the valley. Walk signposted from canal bridge on north side of river.

Canal Exhibition Centre, Llangollen.
Models and films tell the story of growth and use of canals. Horse drawn barge trips. On canal just across road from main bridge.

Railway Station, Llangollen.
Home of Llangollen Railway Society, with a collection of steam engines. By bridge across river.

Valle Crucis Abbey, 1½ miles east of Llangollen on A542 to Ruthin. Substantial remains in a fine setting.

Eliseg's Pillar
Pillar tells story of Eliseg, 1,000 years old. ½ mile up valley from Valle Crucis Abbey.

Horse Shoe Pass, on A542 Ruthin Road, 5 miles north of Llangollen. Steep climb with good views, acquired by National Trust.

Horse Shoe Falls
On River Dee 1 mile east of town centre.

can be taken along the gorge on to the moorland and forests above. If you continue along the road it takes you out on to the open moorland, mainly sheep grazing land, before finally discending to the old lead mining community of Minera.

The River Dee is at its wildest above Llangollen as it descends rapidly from just below the Horseshoe Falls in a series of small cataracts that tumble between the narrow banks — the venue of an annual canoe race. The Horseshoe Falls were built by Telford in 1806 to feed water into a spur of the Shropshire Union Canal running alongside and above the river before crossing 120ft above the river on the 1,000ft-long Pont Cysyllte Aqueduct three miles down river from Llangollen.

About two miles to the north east of Llangollen on the road to Ruthin before it crosses the Horseshoe Pass, is Valle Crucis Abbey, beautifully situated in the centre of what must have been an idyllic valley. The extensive ruins of the church and some of the domestic buildings now almost surrounded by a caravan site, give an idea of the abbey's former size. It was founded by Madog of Gruffyd in 1201 for the Cistercian Order, dissolved in 1535, and now stands to remind us of

Canoeing below the bridge in Llangollen

23

Canal boats near Pont Cysyllte

Valle Crucis Abbey

its former beauty.

The abbey is believed to have taken its name from the pillar standing about ½mile to the north, Eliseg's Pillar, which stands on a mound. Now well worn, it was carved with a Latin inscription in memory of Eliseg who reclaimed Powys (now Clwyd) from the English in the eighth century. Perhaps Eliseg is buried under the mound.

The A5 trunk road, another of Telford's wonders, stretches from London to Holyhead and has been for more than a century and a half the main access to North Wales from England and the south. Running along the bottom of the Vale of Llangollen it provides many of the best views of the river and the surrounding hills. On the north side, the hills lean away from the road and are heather clad in summer, but to the south the hills are heavily afforested and seem to become more so every year. Rising steeply from the very back of Llangollen the road to Llanarmon Glyn Ceiriog and Llanarmon Dyffryn-Ceiriog takes one into some of the most beautiful countryside in North Wales. The narrow lanes meander steeply up and down the deep valleys as forests and hills vie for attention. Such a large area of Wales seems seldom to be visited and it has none of the trappings associated with tourism. It is bounded on the east side by the A5 and Chirk, with its famous castle, and on the west side by the River Dee. The area is crossed by only one road — fortunately an ancient trackway unusable by anything but Landrover type vehicles — but what a splendid route it is, going right over the ridge between Llanarmon Dyffryn-Ceiriog and Llandrillo, crossing the pass below Cadair Bronwen.

These hills, the Berwyns, provide some of the best walking for many miles and can be recommended for experienced walkers as one of the quietest and least frequented parts of North Wales, but one of the most easily accessible. The long ridge walk from Moel Fferna in the north, over the Berwyns to Moel Sych in the south is well worth while, but a map and compass will be essential.

Much of the countryside was explored by the intrepid George Borrow in the 1850s, as he walked many of the lanes and visited many of the villages. One of the towns he describes with little enthusiasm is Llanrhaedr-ym-Mochnant, home of Bishop William Morgan who made the first translation of the Bible into Welsh during the reign of Elizabeth I. Upstream from the village at the head of a steep sided valley is Pistyll Rhaiadr, the highest waterfall in Wales. Now largely surrounded by trees, it is difficult appreci-

Pistyll Rhaiadr – the highest waterfall in Wales

Stone Circle high above Llandrillo

M
1-5h
**
oo

ate the drop of 240ft from a distance. There is however a small car park by a quaint old farmhouse at the end of the lane and after a short walk one can see the full height from a bridge over the stream. The more intrepid walker can continue to the top of the falls by a steep footpath, starting from a grey gate opposite the farm, which zig zags up one side to the top, though this is a rather airy viewpoint. A walk upstream takes one into some fine country — the hills are wild, the ridge walks superb and the scenery splendid: but paths are rare, so go prepared.

To the east, the Berwyns drop slowly down to the River Dee as it casually meanders through the farming and forestry communities of Llandrillo and Cynwyd. Above Llandrillo on the slopes of Cadair Bronwen is a stone circle about 40ft in diameter. What its purpose and origin was we shall probably never know, but whoever placed it there chose the spot well

for the views of the hills and the valley and the feeling of spaciousness are outstanding. It was an ideal place for religious meetings if that was its purpose.

Joining the Afon Alwen, the River Dee turns east towards Llangollen, passing the market town of Corwen on its way. To the north the Llantysilio Mountains above Corwen are crowned by the Iron Age fort of Caer Drewyn. The heather-clad slopes run north east to the top of the Horseshoe Pass, where the remains of the once thriving slate industry scar the landscape.

The mountains are crossed here by the main Llangollen to Ruthin road and there is a viewpoint at the head of the pass looking down towards the Valle Crucis Abbey and Llangollen. As the friendly sheep always seem to be hungry, car doors should be kept firmly closed. The Llantysilio Mountains continue eastwards to the Eglwyseg Mountains, which curve round to the Llandegla Moors to join the Clwydian Range, which eventually terminates in the limestone quarries above Prestatyn on the north coast.

Offa's Dyke follows the line of these hills. From Chepstow in South Wales, it follows roughly the present border until it crosses the River Dee downstream from Llangollen, before climbing up and over Eglwyseg Mountain to World's End and then heads north west along the hills to Prestatyn. It is now a designated long distance footpath of 167 miles and, though a shadow of its former self, can still be seen in several parts of these hills. At one time its massive earthwork was 20ft-wide, with a bank on one side 12ft high, and was probably designed more as a deterrent than an effective barrier, though the actual hills themselves must have been a daunting prospect. Wales is probably more Welsh to the west of it than to the east, and it is on the western side that the Welsh-speaking parts generally lie.

The main road (A494) from Chester to Corwen is one of the main access routes to North Wales and cuts across this range of hills from Mold through Loggerheads, a popular area for short walks, before crossing the shoulder of Moel Famau and dropping into the Vale of Clwyd at Ruthin.

Ruthin or Rudd — meaning Red Fortress — is built on a small hill above the River Clwyd. It is notable for the remains of the castle, built above a red sandstone cliff near the centre of the town. The town probably grew around the castle, which was strategically placed to watch over the river and the road which even in those days was one of the main routes from England. The original Welsh castle build by Prince Llewelyn's brother, Dafydd, was taken by Edward I in 1282 during the Welsh uprising and remained in English hands until dis-

Places of Interest in Ruthin and Corwen

Court House, Ruthin
Black and white building in town centre. Now a bank.

Exmewe Hall, Ruthin
Home of Thomas Exmewe later Lord Mayor of London. Also in town centre.

Maen Huail
Large stone in front of Exmewe Hall on which King Arthur beheaded Huail, his rival in love.

Ruthin Castle, Ruthin
Set in parklands close to the town centre, some ruins but also a hotel holding medieval banquets.

Church of St Peter, Ruthin
Magnificent panelled roof given by Henry VII to men of Wales.

Orissor Craft Centre, Corwen
Old workhouse, well converted, variety of crafts available; you can try you hand at many. On A5 at east side of town.

mantled as a Royalist stronghold by General Mytton in 1647 during the Civil War. Ruthin Castle now houses a luxury hotel specialising in medieval banquets.

A recently built by-pass has eased the congestion in the narrow streets and open square of the town centre. Two banks occupy the notable buildings on the main square. To the south a fine old black and white building is the former Court House dating from 1401, which served as both prison and courthouse. A short beam which was

*Ruthin Town Centre showing the Old Court
House and Exmewe Hall*

once the gallows still projects below the eaves. On the west side is the sixteenth-century Exmewe Hall in front of which is the Maen Huail, a stone on which King Arthur is said to have beheaded Huail, his rival in love. The hall was built by Thomas Exmewe, who later became Lord Mayor of London.

The Church of St Peter stands to the north east of the square. At one time it was a collegiate church, and dates in parts from the thirteenth and fourteenth centuries. The interior has a magnificent oak panelled roof, made of 500 carved panels, every one different, which was presented to all the men of Wales by Henry VII for their help in gaining the throne for him.

The remains of Iron Age hillforts and barrows on the hilltops around the town show signs of earlier habitation.

The hills here are certainly more friendly than those further west in Snowdonia: perhaps this attracted the old tribes. Today they are crossed by many roads, from which many walks can be enjoyed along the good network of footpaths, with an Ordnance Survey map.

3 Clwyd-The Coast and Inland

Clwyd was formed in 1974 during local government re-organisation as an amalgamation of the two counties Flintshire and Denbighshire and is part of the old Welsh region of Gwynedd. It takes its most recent name from the River Clwyd which bisects the county, and is bounded on its eastern side by England and the River Dee, while its other boundary runs a few miles east of the River Conwy. For this chapter a more logical boundary is the River Conwy.

The area has two main attractions for the visitor: the inland hills for walkers and sightseers, and the beautiful beaches on the northern coast for those who like a more relaxing day.

The coastlands are flat: there is a choice of roads from Queensferry, either the inland route, the A55, or the more scenic coast road the A548, giving easy access to all the resorts. On both routes there are many reminders of the area's turbulent history, particularly of Edward I's attempts to subdue

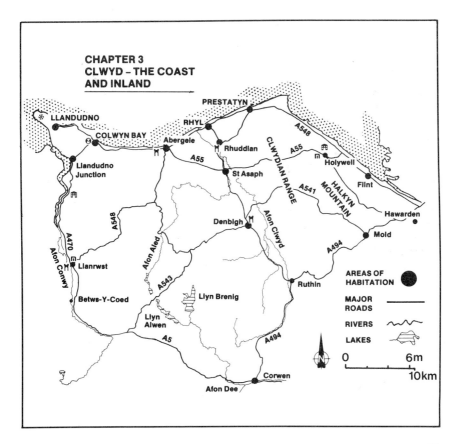

CHAPTER 3
CLWYD – THE COAST
AND INLAND

the Welsh princes in the late thirteenth century, when he built castles at all strategic points to maintain law and order. There are many fine ruins from this 'ring of steel' for the visitor to enjoy, most of them only slightly off the beaten track.

After crossing the River Dee at Queensferry or Chester the coastal road runs through some of the most depressing scenery in the whole of the county, as it follows for many miles the culmination of hundreds of years of industrialisation. Though the sea is never more than a mile away, it is only glimpsed occasionally between the mammoth buildings, many of which are now redundant. Fortunately this industrial zone is limited to a very narrow belt, backing on to the estuary, and can be easily avoided by using the inland route.

Inevitably, after conquering Wales, Edward I built a fortification on the first high ground after Chester. He chose the site of an Iron Age fort at Hawarden and there built a stone castle with a round tower. Some parts remain today, but much of it was destroyed by the Parliamentarians in 1646. A later house started in 1750, still standing below the castle, was the home of one of Queen Victoria's Prime Ministers, William Gladstone, who acquired the estate when he married Catherine Glynne. He lived there for sixty years and the neat little village bears many reminders of this most famous resident. There is a Gladstone museum, a window and an effigy in the church almost opposite the main gates to the estate, and a statue also near the gates. Next to the church in Hawarden is the Deiniol Library founded by Gladstone in 1895, and housing a collection of theological books and pamphlets which are available for study.

Just two miles away from Edward's

castle at Hawarden stand the remains of Ewloe Castle, now surrounded by trees and barely visible from the road. It was built by Llewelyn the Last about 1260 and is typical of a Welsh stone castle, built to provide a buffer between the warring English and Welsh.

It is difficult now to imagine the importance of this area in past times; it was the main route into Wales from Chester and England, for the hills further inland were inhospitable and dangerous to cross. The coastal belt formed the main highway for all the invading armies from the Romans onwards. As it is also easier to supply armies by sea than over land, the area has therefore always been strategically important.

To complement the castle at Hawarden which guarded the inland route, Edward I built a fortress at Flint to protect the coastal route and the estuary of the River Dee. The castle, built on rock on the very edge of the sands, is all that remains of a once walled town. It is just off the main square and missed by the many visitors who head each year for the beaches further along the coast. One tower is

---

Things to See Around Mold

Daniel Owen Centre, Early Road, Mold
Exhibition centre of local arts and memorial museum to Daniel Owen, one of Wales's leading novelist.

Theatr Clwyd, Mold
Three theatres under one roof, regular programme of films, concerts and live exhibitions. Has its own professional company. Close to town centre.

detached from the main body of the castle and is connected by a draw-bridge; it is the only example of this in the country. The tower or donjon was to be the last line of defence. The castle was the scene of the betrayal of Richard II and was immortalised in Shakespeare's play, much of which is set there. Today the castle is almost surrounded by buildings, and the Dee continues to silt up. The port that flourished until the last century no longer exists and today the town relies on modern industry for its survival.

The new county town is Mold, just five miles to the south of Flint. Unlike its predecessor it occupies a position of no particular geographical or his-torical importance, though it is a very pleasant little town. There was a small Norman Castle on Bailey Hill at one end of the High Street, and the church, which is fifteenth century, has some fine stained glass windows and friezes carved with animals.

Mold was the home in the nineteeth century of Daniel Owen, a novelist and short story writer, who wrote in the Welsh language about Welsh people. He was a tailor who spent most of his life in the town. There is now a small museum at the Daniel Owen Centre containing memorabilia of this fine author.

Each Saturday, the main street in Mold is closed for the market, the stalls of which are set up on each side of the road. Perhaps of less interest to the visitor but more noticeable by its size is the new administrative buildings of Clwyd County Council which are about half a mile from the town centre on the Chester road. There too is the Theatr Clwyd, a centre for entertain-ment and arts. There are regular concerts, and the theatre has its own professional company.

On the opposite side of the town the A494 Ruthin road rises steeply to the Rainbow Inn, before dropping even more steeply down to the Loggerheads Inn at the bottom of a deeply wooded valley. There is a car park here and short walks can be taken along the valley and through the woods, — a pleasant spot to spend an afternoon. There are some steep limestone cliffs above the woods which give a feeling of depth to this little valley.

L
1-1½h
*
oo

Continuing along the main Ruthin road a minor road, probably the original road, turns off to the right about one mile after Loggerheads. If one takes this to the top of the pass and parks for a short while there are some breathtaking views over Ruthin and the Vale of Clwyd, to the north and the sea. From the parking spot there is a good footpath leading up to the Jubilee Tower on the summit of Moel Famau. The tower was built to commemorate George III's jubilee. It is now part of a country park and on a clear day one can sometimes see the Isle of Man and the mountains of the Lake District to the north; but the closer views of Snowdonia to the west are more rewarding. It is a pleasant stroll, well worth doing. From the car park the single track road descends steeply into Ruthin and requires care.

M
1-2h
*
ooo

To the north of Mold is Halkyn Mountain which runs nearly parallel with the estuary. It is composed mainly of limestone and for many centuries was the source of much of the wealth of the county; it was riddled with lead and lead mines. There are many remains of engine houses and tunnels of interest to the industrial archaeologist. The Romans mined here but it was the nineteenth-century entrepreneurs who used their technology to sink even deeper mines and longer tunnels. Water seepage was always a serious problem and it was not until 1878 that a tunnel almost the full length of the mountain drained the mines into the estuary.

Today the hill is extensively quarried for the limestone, but for walkers there are excellent views across the Dee estuary, the Wirral and the Mersey estuary to Liverpool and the Lancashire plain.

On the northern slopes of Halkyn Mountain stands the small town of Holywell, once a centre for many pilgrims. The well is said to have curative powers and is part of St Winifred's Chapel, a perpendicular church built by Margaret Beaufort, the mother of Henry VII. Pilgrims enter the bath by steps, and kneel to pray on the stone of St Beuno, founder of an earlier chapel on the site. The Holy Well was originally fed by a spring from the nearby limestone hills, but since the early part of this century has been fed by a small reservoir. Until the Reformation, the well was in the care of the Cistercian monks from nearby Basingwerk Abbey. The abbey, just one mile north east of Holywell, in a beautiful setting, was known for its fine building and windows. It was taken apart at the Dissolution and the present remains, which are mainly thirteenth century (though the original abbey was founded in 1132), give some idea of the extent of the building.

Modern visitors in the summer will be content to by-pass the towns backing the Dee Estuary and speed west along the coast to the seaside towns and caravan sites which for many are the attractions in this part of Wales. From the colliery at the Point of Ayr the fields bordering the coastal road become a continuous mass of caravan sites and holiday camps which from Easter onwards attract visitors from all over Britain. It is a popular area for family holidays and weekend visitors, as there are many fine beaches along this northern coast which are safe for bathing and boating.

Prestatyn, the first major town to be reached, is a pleasant place with three main beaches and two large holiday camps. Ffrith beach, the most northerly, has convenient parking, a play area with motor boats, a mini-golf course and other amusements. Central Beach has the Royal Lido Centre backing onto it, a heated swimming pool if the sea is too cold, band concerts and bars. Barkby Beach is perhaps a little quieter and has access for boat trailers. Central and Ffrith Beaches are the best for bathing.

The town itself is a thriving community all the year round with many residents, and does not rely solely on summer visitors for its livelihood. There is a good range of shops, cafes and hotels. Inland from the coast is an 18-hole golfcourse at Meliden. Above Meliden is a range of limestone hills with several short walks which give excellent views all along the coast. Above Prestatyn on the road out to

---

Things to See Around Holywell

St Winifred's Chapel, Holywell
Built by Margaret Beaufort, mother of Henry VII, it houses the Holy Well. A centre for pilgrims for centuries.

Basingwerk Abbey, off A548, 1 mile north of Holywell
Praised for its beauty and setting. Ruins fairly extensive.

Military Museum, off the A55, ¾ mile west of Holywell
Housed in an underground cavern is a large collection of military vehicles, weapons and medals. Picnic area, parking and café.

The Sun Centre, Rhyl

L
1h
*
oo

Gwaenysgor, there is a small car park before the road climbs steeply; the signpost shows the route to Offa's Dyke Path and a walk through the woods up to the top of the hills. This is the northern end of the Offa's Dyke Path mentioned in the previous chapter. Crowning the hill are the embankments of an old Iron Age fort. Just to the south at Gop Hill are some caves where remains of Stone Age man have been found. For the archaeologist this area is particularly fascinating, for there is much evidence of prehistoric man.

Rhyl is only four miles from Prestatyn, but seems much more on a busy Sunday when the traffic moves slowly. Perhaps the most famous seaside town in North Wales, catering for many thousands of visitors each year, it differs completely from its near neighbour and is so much more brash. There is something for everybody — all the necessary seaside amusements on the promenade, and a beach which is excellent for swimming, though one must take care at the western end near the mouth of the River Clwyd. Most of the major attractions are along the sea front on the wide promenade. The Sun Centre dominates the Eastern Parade, a large modern structure mainly of glass containing restaurants amusements, a swimming pool with a wave-making machine and other swimming pools.

Further along is the Flora Hall, well known for its magnificent displays of flowers, a paddling pool, bandstand, and the Ocean Beach park with its roundabouts and all-the-fun-of-the-fair. Alongside is the Marine Lake for boating.

The River Clwyd with its once wide estuary and reclaimed marshland effectively forms the western boundary of the town, but the road continues parallel with the sea through the fields of caravans to Abergele, just four miles further on. This small town seems to be more Welsh than its neighbour; at the junction of several main roads, its narrow streets are always busy. It is a market town and the old church contains some interesting relics of the past, with some fifteenth and sixteenth century glass and a dug-out chest. The churchyard has two memorials to disasters which happened in the neighbourhood, a shipwreck and a train crash.

Although situated about one mile from the seashore, Abergele, now joined to Pensarn on the coast, with its pebbly beaches and sandhills, is a pleasant town for a more relaxing day.

On the outskirts of the town are the long walls and great gatehouse surrounding Gwrych Castle, set below wooded hills in a large estate. It is an impressive site, though unfortunately a folly, for the castle was built in 1815 by a wealthy tycoon. It is open to the public and contains many antiques and fine furnishings. The parklands contain an amusement centre which has a miniature railway and holds jousting contests on summer afternoons. There are several short walks in the surrounding woodlands.

The main road, now a dual carriageway for much of its length, speeds up and over the headland to Penmaen-Rhos with its huge limestone quarries, and then drops steeply into the back of Colwyn Bay.

Before the descent there is a fine viewpoint beside the main road where the sweep of the bay around the Little Orme can be seen. The whole shoreline has beautiful sandy beaches with a promenade running almost the full curve of the bay.

Colwyn Bay, with its neighbour Rhos-on-Sea, has mushroomed in recent years to become a major holiday resort. Besides all the usual attractions along the promenade, including a pier, it has much to offer and many places of interest. Eirias Park runs south from the promenade, with picnic areas, boating, bowls, tennis and a sports area. The nearby Prince of Wales Theatre has a busy summer season with a variety of shows ,while in Rhos there is the Harlequin Puppet Theatre, an open air swimming pool just off the promenade and a golf course.

A curiosity on the seashore at Rhos is the miniature church of St Trillo

Gwyrch Castle (near Abergele) – not as old as it lookst looks

built over a small well. The chapel is only 11ft by 8ft and is probably the smallest in Wales. Its age is unknown and its purpose vague, but local people say fishermen and sailors prayed there before a journey. Services are now held outside.

On the outskirts of the town is the famous Welsh Mountain Zoo where a

---

What to See Around Abergele

Abergele Beach
Pebble but sand as the tide recedes. Popular for caravans.

Gwrych Castle
Mock castle built in beautiful setting. Fine furniture inside, with jousting and miniature railway in grounds. Just off A55 outside, west of Abergele.

---

wide variety of birds and animals are kept in as near natural surroundings a possible. There are many birds of prey, and weather permitting, daily flying displays of eagles, falcons, etc. Behind Rhos-on-Sea is the small hill of Bryn Euryn. Although almost surrounded by roads it is nevertheless a pleasant place to stroll and to enjoy the panoramic views over the towns and bay.

L
1h
*
oo

The road climbs over the shoulder of the Little Orme and then descends to follow the promenade to Llandudno, sheltered on a neck of land by the massive bulk of the Great Orme. The town straddles the low lying land with the main amusement centres on the north-facing coast and the quieter residential areas overlooking the estuary of the River Conwy. The town retains much of its Victorian grandeur and gives the impression of being more conservative than its neighbours.

Colwyn Bay and the Little Orme

The promenade follows the curve of the bay and has most of the usual amusements. At the foot of the Great Orme is the Pier Pavilion. Attached is a landing stage for steamers which offer trips around the bay, along the coast and even to the Isle of Man. There are several theatres in the town attracting first class variety acts during the summer months, and it is best to enquire locally for the current attractions. Happy Valley is a public park where everybody should be made to smile; it has playgrounds, rockpools and an open air theatre. From the park a cabin lift leaves for the summit of the Great Orme. Llandudno is not only an amusement centre: it has many fine shops in the main street. Rapallo House about a mile from the town centre is a museum and art gallery with many displays relating to Welsh history.

On the other side of the town, the West Shore, overlooking the Conwy estuary and Snowdonia, is generally

Places to Visit Around Colwyn Bay

Colwyn Beach
A long curving beach, round the bay. Good sand and safe bathing, very popular

Eirias Park
Boating, bowls, tennis, picnic spots.

Prince of Wales Theatre
Regular variety shows, bands and plays

Welsh Mountain Zoo
Collection of animals and birds of prey with free flying displays daily (weather permitting). Off A55 by West End Shopping Centre.

Rhos-on-Sea
Extension of Colwyn Bay, with Harlequin Puppet Theatre, open-air swimming pool (heated), and St Trillo's church on the beach

Llandudno and the Great Orme

Places of Interest Around Llandudno

Beaches
North Shore: Good beach backed by Promenade. Safe bathing, launch facilities and water skiing area.
West Shore: Shingle beach, sea goes out a long way at low tide, so bathing is only when tide is in.

Great Orme
Nature trails, tramway and cabin lift to summit

Happy Valley
Park with playground, rock gardens and the open air theatre.

Pier
With Theatre and landing stage

Rapallo House
Museum and arts centre with exhibits of local and national interest.

Bodnant Gardens
Beautiful gardens and woodlands, some of the finest in Europe. 6 miles south of Llandudno Junction off A470.

Felin Isaf Llansantffraid, Glan Conwy.
Seventeenth-century flour mill with original machinery and methods.

Lewis Carroll Memorial,
West Shore, Llandudno

quieter. It was here that Charles Dodgson (Lewis Carroll) spent several holidays at the house of Dean Liddell, whose daughter inspired the tales of Alice in Wonderland. A memorial portraying the White Rabbit from those tales was unveiled there in 1933 by Lloyd George.

The Great Orme dominates Llandudno and no doubt protects it from the prevailing westerly winds. A toll road (Marine Drive) encircles the headland, giving some fine views of the cliffs and caves and coast to the south. It is possible to reach the summit cafe (679ft) by car, foot, tramway or cabin lift. The latter two are a continuous daily service during the summer months. There are many minor antiquities on the hillsides and the Great Orme Nature Trail which starts in the Happy Valley is perhaps the best way to see them. It is also an excellent way of escaping from the hustle and bustle for a few hours and enjoying this magnificent setting.

A short distance to the south of Llandudno and standing on the shores of the Conwy estuary is Deganwy. With its castle, now only a ruin, it has for many centuruies guarded the northern entrance to the River Conwy. Today, with a sheltered harbour, it is a popular resort and centre for sailing.

L
1-2h
*
ooo

38

One of its best attractions is Bodnant Gardens, the home of Lord Aberconwy, five miles to the south of Deganwy. It is one of the finest gardens in Britain, well known for its wonderful collection of trees from all over the world. There are sixty acres of formal and informal gardens on the hillside overlooking the mountains of Snowdonia.

Up river from Bodnant, squeezed between the steep hills and the meandering river, is Llanrwst, a solid Welsh market town, It is a town little altered by tourism, that serves a wide community in the surrounding hills and forests. The River Conwy has many outstanding bridges, not least of which is the beautiful arched bridge here. Said to have been built by Inigo Jones in 1636, it was commissioned by the Wynn family who lived in Gwydir Castle on the opposite bank. There are other reminders of this wealthy family in the old church off the town square.

The hills between Llanrwst and the coast to the north are green and round. The deep valleys are full of trees and are a sharp contrast to the bigger, more sombre, mountains across the valley. There are many small villages nestling in the valleys but the area generally is neglected by most visitors.

The moors to the south, stretching almost to the Vale of Clwyd, are well known for their grouse shooting. Many of the high reservoirs offer facilities for sailing and angling. The largest, Llyn Brenig, 8 miles south of Denbigh, has a visitors' centre and several planned walks to local archaeological sites: it is also a bird sanctuary and has some pleasant picnic spots. This is a huge area of countryside backing on to the coast and well worth exploring as an alternative to relaxing on the beach.

To the east is the historic former county town of Denbigh, built a short distance above the river. The castle, built by Henry de Lacy in 1282 for Edward I to help maintain law and order in the region, changed hands frequently between the Welsh and the English. It was finally destroyed by the Roundheads in 1645 after an eleven-month siege; Charles I had taken refuge there after his defeat at Rowton Moor near Chester. It has a large and beautiful gatehouse and some interesting defensive ideas built in, though little now remains. Nearby are the walls of Leicester's Church begun by the Earl of Leicester in 1579 to replace St Asaph's Cathedral, but never completed. The remains of the town walls to the north of this ruin show how important Denbigh was in the past.

H. M. Stanley, the adventurer and the author of the remark 'Doctor Livingstone, I presume' was born in Denbigh, and Sir Hugh Myddleton, who constructed London's water supply in the reign of James I lived close by at Gwaunynog. Thomas Edwards a famous and well loved bard, and the author known as Twm o'r Nant, is buried in the parish church one mile east of the town.

Downstream from Denbigh is the cathedral town of St Asaph. Though the cathedral is perhaps less famous nowadays than the nearby white 'marble' church at Bodelwyddan it gives the place the status of a city, the smallest (as is the cathedral) in Great Britain. The cathedral is a squat building on the site of a church founded in AD560 by St Mungo, who was succeeded in AD573 by St Asaph, from whom the town takes its name. There has been a cathedral here ever since, despite Edward I's attempts to build an alternative at Rhuddlan. The present, much restored, building contains many features that have survived from earlier centuries. The Chapter Museum contains a fine collection of early religious manuscripts and bibles, but it is open only by request and never on Sundays.

Three miles to the north is Rhuddlan Castle, perhaps one of the most solid-looking of all Edward's castles. It stands on the banks of the Clwyd, which was diverted and canalised to allow ships to sail in from the sea and berth at high tide. It guarded the main coastal route into North Wales and stands as a grim reminder to modern visitors of the troubled past of this land. Many people pass through Rhuddlan each year, but few realise that the valley to the south played such an important part in shaping the future of the Welsh people.

Rhuddlan Castle

4 The Northern Mountains of Gwyedd

Some visitors will perhaps explore only the resorts on the northern coast, but it is the mountains west of the River Conwy that are the attraction to many others. Rising steeply from the banks of the river, they contain some of the highest peaks in England and Wales as well as some of the oldest. They are visible for many miles, and form a jagged skyline in sharp contrast to the surrounding moorlands.

For convenience we shall consider the larger towns and villages first, for the hills are to a great extent the domain of the experienced climber and hillwalker, though there are several interesting excursions on foot for the novice. All the large towns are situated on the coast and events have shown how important the routes along the coastal belt have been in the past. To the modern traveller they are equally important, for they are the normal access routes for most people approaching from the north and north-west of England. After passing through Abergele both coastal roads become one busy main road (A55), threading through Colwyn Bay and Llandudno Junction to arrive at one of the main crossing points of the River Conwy.

There are three bridges across the Conwy estuary: Stephenson's tubular railway bridge, Telford's beautiful suspension bridge now used only by pedestrians, and a modern road bridge which unfortunately has turned one of the most attractive historic towns in North Wales into a bottleneck for traffic during much of the summer.

The town of Conwy is situated on the very edge of the estuary with the superbly sited castle dominating the town from its rocky perch above the river. It is one of the most interesting, and probably one of the most visited, towns in Wales. The walls surrounding the town are almost complete and with the castle form a unique defensive work. The enclosed narrow streets are as busy as the quay and landing stage. All contribute to make the town a popular holiday and yachting centre.

The castle stands on the site of a Cistercian monastery built in the tenth century, but uprooted 100 years later and moved to Maenan 5 miles upstream by Edward I, who saw the site as more suitable for defence than religion. The castle was built in only four years, a remarkable feat without modern mechanical aids, and served in part as a royal palace. During its stormy lifetime it has regularly changed hands between the Welsh and English before finally being captured and dismantled by the Parliamentarian under General Mytton in 1646.

Modern visitors to the castle approach from Castle Square and it is from high on its walls that the best views of the nearby hills and the town walls can be seen. The walls were built at the same time as the castle and are part of an integral defensive scheme for the town; they follow the rise and fall of the land and are approximately 30ft-tall with twenty-one towers throughout their length.

The quay is within the walls and has long been a port for fishing boats. Today it is becoming more important as a centre for yachtsmen and boating enthusiasts, the harbour providing a safe mooring. It is a busy place, full of

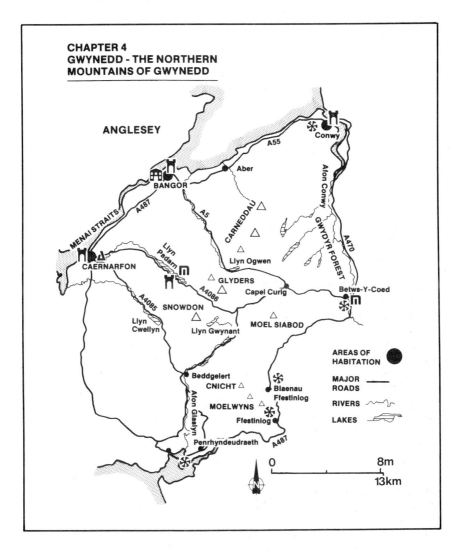

ANGLESEY

Conwy

A55

Aber

BANGOR

Afon Conwy

MENAI STRAITS

A487

A5

CARNEDDAU

GWYDYR FOREST

A470

Llyn Ogwen

CAERNARFON

Llyn Padarn

GLYDERS

Capel Curig

Betws-Y-Coed

A4086

SNOWDON

A4085

Llyn Cwellyn

Llyn Gwynant

MOEL SIABOD

AREAS OF HABITATION

Beddgelert

CNICHT

Blaenau Ffestiniog

MAJOR ROADS

Afon Glaslyn

MOELWYNS

RIVERS

Ffestiniog

LAKES

Penrhyndeudraeth

A487

0   8m

13km

N

hustle and bustle, though still a pleasant place to sit and watch the world go by. On the quayside is Britain's smallest house, a tiny half-up and half-down, built by a bachelor who obviously intended to remain so.

Plas Mawr is perhaps the next most visited building to the castle, a fine example of an Elizabethan building; just off the High Street, it has many interesting features both inside and outside. It is now an art gallery housing the annual exhibition of the Royal Cambrian Academy of Art. Lower down the High Street, Aberconwy is a white timber and stone house owned by the National Trust, and a fine reminder of the type of town house built in the fifteenth and sixteenth centuries.

Almost surrounded by houses and streets stands St Mary's church which occupies the site of the early Cistercian abbey. Much of the exterior

Conwy Castle and suspension bridge. The bridge was built by Telford

structure is part of the original abbey, but the centuries have seen many additions to both inside and outside, and it is now a good example of the development of a parish church through the years.

Behind the town are some good uphill walks with clear paths, particularly over Conwy Mountain (only 808ft high) to the Iron Age hillfort of Caer Leion. The old road crossed the Sychnant Pass behind Conwy to the coast at Penmaenmawr, and the head of the pass is a good place to park

Conwy Walls

Places of Interest in and Around Conwy

Plas Mawr, High Street, Conwy
Perfect example of an Elizabethan building. Now houses Royal Cambrian Academy of Art

Conwy Castle and Walls
Magnificent setting, best example in country

Aberconwy House
A good example of a fourteenth-century timber framed house

St Mary's Church
Originally part of Cistercian Abbey but developed as a parish church over the years

Smallest House
Literally that on the quayside

Conwy Mountain
Hut circles and footpaths in most directions

Sychnant Pass
Old road connecting Conwy and Penmaenmawr

before enjoying one of the many short (or long) walks on the nearby slopes.

The river and the lakes upstream from Conwy are the breeding grounds for salmon. Several local families are licensed to catch the fish as they swim upstream, using nets which must not be below a particular mesh size, ensuring that only the larger fish are caught.

The modern road westwards from Conwy hugs the coast through a series of tunnels to give a smooth, quick ride through Penmaenmawr to Bangor. The old road over Sychnant Pass had a formidable reputation and many travellers preferred to walk along the shoreline than cross the pass. Frequently the road was so bad that the carriage had to be dismantled to get it over the worst parts.

The hills to the south of the old and new roads have many reminders of the prehistoric men who inhabited the area. Just above Penmaenmawr at Craig Lwyd was a stone axe factory.

Using the tough granite, Stone Age man chipped and shaped it, both for his own use and for 'export'; axes from the site have been found all over the country. There are many other prehistoric sites, some of which have been combined into a history trail from Penmaenmawr; leaflets are available in local shops.

L
1-2h
*
ooo

Modern man still finds the granite worth quarrying, the summit of Penmaenmawr, from which the town gets its name, being a major source of this material; the height of the hill is reduced annually.

Aber, a short distance further on, is

45

Smallest House, Conwy

a small village best known for the waterfall in the hills above. One turns off the main road and parks at the car park at the end of the valley. A walk of about 1 mile up the valley leads to the most impressive falls, which have a vertical drop of about 120ft. To the west are the smaller cataracts of Afon Bach. The hills south of the falls are owned by the National Trust, and the mountains of the Carneddau are some of the wildest and highest in Snowdonia. Aber's car park is an ideal starting point for walks into these hills, but only experienced walkers, able to use a map and compass, should consider such an expedition.

The coast road continues south to join the A5 trunk road at Llandegai. This busy road from London to Holyhead was built by Thomas Telford in the early nineteenth century to speed the journey to and from Ireland. Opposite the junction is Penrhyn Castle and estate, now run by the National Trust. Until recently it was the home of the Pennant family who were the former owners of the Penrhyn Slate quarries in Bethesda. The house, which overlooks the Menai Straits, is a masterpiece of neo-Norman architecture and for obvious reasons slate has been used extensively both inside and outside.

The style and ostentatious design of the building reflect the unlimited amount of money available to many nineteenth century businessmen. Parts of the building now house a doll museum, and on the estate is an industrial railway museum. In the old days, most of the slate shipped from the quarries went from the quay on the estate, so that the owner and management could keep a close eye on the amount being sold and despatched.

Bangor, one of the five university towns of Wales, stands at the northern end of the Menai Straits, most of the town being squeezed between two low hills in a shallow valley. It is dominated by the buildings of the University College of North Wales which stand on the hill between the town and the Straits. The University is perhaps modern Bangor's main claim to fame, though in the past it has been the Celtic centre for Christanity: a bishopric was established as long ago as AD546.

The cathedral is thought to be the oldest in Britain in continuous use. The building, though not remarkable, has seen continuous development since Norman times and, despite suffering much at the hands of both Welsh and English aggressors, bears much evidence of the many phases of its development. Nearby is the old Bishop's Palace, built mainly in the sixteenth century and now the town hall. Almost opposite is the Theatr Gwynedd, the centre for the perform-

Places of Interest in and around Bangor

Penrhyn Castle
An elegant neo-Norman mansion on the edge of the Menai Straits; many slate artefacts in the building. Just off the A55 north of Bangor.

Theatr Gwynedd
County centre for theatre and films with regular performances.

Bangor Cathedral
Thought to be the oldest in Britain, shows evidence of continuous development since sixth century.

Old Canonry, Bangor
Houses Museum of Welsh Antiquities, with collection of seventeenth century furniture illustrating Welsh rural crafts. Pre-historic and Romano-British objects

ing arts in the county.

The Museum of Welsh Antiquities, housed in the Old Canonry near the cathedral, contains exhibits from prehistoric, Roman and more recent times giving a good background to the development of the town, surrounding area and Wales generally. The city was a quiet religious centre until early last century. The opening of the two bridges across the Menai Straits in the first half of the nineteenth century resulted in increased traffic by road and rail through the town. With the arrival of the University College in 1883, Bangor finally became a municipality and busy commercial centre.

At the southern end of the Menai Straits is the historic town of Caernarfon. It is probably the best known of

Caernarfon Castle

all the towns in North Wales, and it stands in a magnificent position at the foot of the mountains overlooking Anglesey. The castle, built by Edward I, is one of the greatest (and most attractive) castles in the country. It stands above the busy quayside as a reminder of the strategic importance of this bustling town. Traditionally the castle is where Edward II was invested as the first Prince of Wales after his birth there in 1284, The castle has in more recent times seen the investitures as Prince of Wales of the future Edward VIII (in 1911) and of Prince Charles (in 1969).

Unusually, the castle has thirteen polygonal towers and banded masonry and although outwardly perfect it is internally just a shell. Like all castles in this region it has had a stormy career, playing a significant part in the wars between the Welsh and English princes. Despite its capture by Cromwell's troops in 1660 it stands now as a magnificent reminder of the castle builder's craft. In the Queen's Tower within the walls is the Museum of the Royal Welch Fusiliers, with many mementoes from the history of the regiment.

As at Conwy, much of the town wall survives, built with the castle as part of an integrated defensive system. It surrounds the old parts of the town, the narrow streets forming a regular pattern within. In the north-west corner, and built into the walls, is the Chantry of St Mary which utilised the adjoining tower as a vestry and bell tower. There are many fine old buildings enclosed by the walls, including the Black Boy Inn, a traditional public house with some good local dishes, and the old Market Hall which now is more a centre for local crafts than a market.

Until very recently the town, like many along the coast, was blighted by

Places of Interest in Caernarfon

Caernarfon Castle
Finest of Edward's castles. Polygonal towers with banded masonry make it unique

Town Walls
Circle inner part of town, part of integral defensive system

Segontium
Roman Fort on outskirts of town. Some buildings to see and a museum showing history of the site.

Market Hall, nr town centre
Now a centre for local crafts and shops

Museum of Royal Welch Fusiliers
Military museum inside castle, with many mementoes of the regiment's past.

traffic, but the building of a new bypass has considerably relieved the congestion, thus allowing visitors to wander at a more leisurely pace than previously. Castle Square, which is now relatively free from traffic, has a Saturday market and is an ideal base to explore the town.

The Romans also appreciated the value of the site's strategic importance, or perhaps they just found it slightly less hostile than the mountains inland. They built a fort just to the south of the present town, half a mile out, on the road to Beddgelert. Little now remains but the foundations give a good idea of the ground plan. On the site is an excellent museum covering the history of the fort and the organization of the Roman army in Britain and other related subjects. The fort, known as *Segontium*, was occupied from about AD78 to AD380 when the Roman troops withdrew from Britain. During that time a sizeable community had grown up outside the walls and on retirement many of the soldiers are believed to have settled and farmed in the area. It had been a fort well integrated with local life.

The view south from Caernarfon and Bangor is of the mountains. They are not large by comparison with other European mountain ranges but they always give an overriding impression of grandeur. They form the northern end of the Snowdonia National Park and are divided into three distinct ranges, separated by deep valleys. To the east, bounded on one side by the Conwy Valley and on the other by the Nant Ffrancon Pass, are the Carneddau; in the centre are the Glyders; and on the west, the highest of all, is Snowdon with its surrounding mountains. In all there are fourteen peaks over 3,000ft, all linked by footpaths.

The mountains, originally formed more than 300 million years ago, are the worn down stumps of much higher mountains. They have been folded by earth movements to more than 20,000ft and then gradually worn by changing temperatures, water and ice to their present size. The valleys have been carved by ancient glaciers and many of the hanging valleys, called cwms, have been dammed by glacial deposits to hold lakes. The debris of glaciers is scattered around the hillsides and in moraines along and across the valleys. The alpine plants left by the receding ice in some of the high cwms provide a living link with the Ice Age and show how little these mountains have changed despite man's interference.

Snowdon is the highest mountain in England and Wales. With its sharp ridges and sombre cwms, it is inevitable that stories have grown around

Crib Goch and the Snowdon Horseshoe

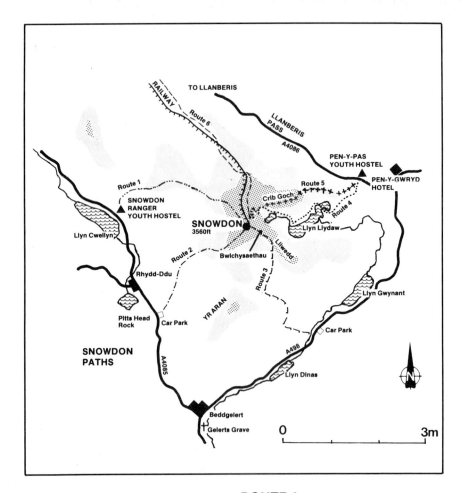

SNOWDON PATHS

ROUTE 1
SNOWDON RANGER TRACK: 3¾ miles. An easy path with delightful views, zig-zags above youth hostel.

ROUTE 2
BEDDGELERT PATH: 3¾ miles. Easy to follow, climbs gradually to summit. Steeper near top.

ROUTE 3
WATKIN TRACK: 3½ miles. Most interesting, but hardest walk. Good path at first up to Bwlch Y Saethau, steep and loose after that.

ROUTE 4
MINER'S TRACK: 3¾ miles. Follows copper miners track to lake, then rises more steeply to join PYG track to summit. Good for introduction to the mountain if you do not wish to go to the top.

ROUTE 5
PYG TRACK: 3¼ miles. Good route. Climbs quickly and then contours around cwm to climb. Zig-zags below summit.

ROUTE 6
LLANBERIS PATH: 5 miles. Follows close to railway. Starts in Llanberis and climb easily. Not the most interesting route.

Snowdon in cloud looking up Watkin Track

it. This is the land of the legendary King Arthur. Yr Wyddfa, the highest peak, is traditionally the tomb of Rhita Fawr slain by Arthur. Arthur is supposed to have fought his last battle at the Pass of Arrows (Bwlch y Saethau) below Snowdon's Summit; Llyn Llydaw therefore is the lake into which Excalibur was thrown. On the slopes above is a cave in which three of King Arthur's knights rest, ready to come to the aid of the country when needed. Despite the legends, what is more certain is that several of the Welsh princes retreated into the area when defeated, for it would prove a most hostile environment to the pursuing English troops.

The Snowdon massif is a star-shaped cluster of five peaks connected by a series of steep ridges; the highest, Yr Wyddfa at 3,560ft, is the centre, and is perhaps the most popular walk or climb in the country. It can be reached by a rack and pinion railway from Llanberis, or by footpath from north, south, east and west. There are easy footpaths past the lakes and through the cwms, or harder ones for only the very experienced along the ridges.

The ascent of the summit, Yr Wyddfa, has been understandably a popular achievement at least from early last century when George Borrow in his book *Wild Wales* describes how he walked up with his family in 1850 and even at that time 'there was a rude cabin in which refreshments are sold and in which a person resides throughout the year'. The modern cafe is an ugly concrete block, serving mainly the trippers on the railway, and open only when the train is running. For much of the year the railway track is blocked by snow and the hotel is closed.

There are six main routes up Snowdon, starting from car parks all around

Things to See and Do Around Llanberis

Snowdon Mountain Railway
Runs a regular passenger service to the summit of Snowdon

Welsh Slate Museum
In the former workshops of Dinorwic Quarry, showing much of the original machinery and equipment used. Films and slides of quarry work.

Llanberis Lake Railway
Steam railway starting from the Quarrying Museum and running along lakeside through country park.

Dolbadarn Castle
Home of the Welsh Princes in the twelfth century, it stands above the lake guarding the entrance to the Llanberis Pass

Padarn Country Park
On shore of the lake with native oak trees and walks through quarry remains.

the mountain. Although some are easier and some are longer, all require much physical effort and a sound knowledge of mountain walking, for the weather can change drastically during the 5-8 hours of the walk. All the paths are well made and quite easy to follow if care is taken.

Perhaps the greatest expedition is the Snowdon Horseshoe, a traverse of all the main peaks to and from Pen-y-Pass. It involves steep climbing and knife-edge ridges following the rim of the cwm surrounding Llyn Llydaw and taking in the summits of Grib-

H
6-7h
****
oooo

Goch (3,023ft), Crib-y-Ddysgl (3,493 ft) over Yr Wyddfa (3,560ft) before descending to Bwlch-y-Saethau and the steep crags of Lliwedd (2,947ft) and thence back down the Miners' Track to Pen-y-Pass. It must be stressed that this is a major undertaking and should not be attempted without a stout pair of boots, a head for heights and much previous experience; the weather and rock conditions should be checked before attempting this marvellous expedition.

Pen-y-Pass, the highest point of the Llanberis Pass, and the starting point for many of the Snowdon Walks, is the site of the old Gorphwysfa Hotel, an old coaching inn converted some years ago to a Youth Hostel. In the early part of the century the old hotel was the centre for the pioneer rock climbers who visited the many crags on the slopes of Snowdon. The road descends steeply from there down to the south east to the Pen y Gwryd Hotel, which superseded it as the meeting place for climbers and became

Llyn Peris and the Llanberis Pass

Across Llyn Peris with slate waste and outflow from the Dinorwic Pumped storage scheme

particularly famous after the first successful Mount Everest climbers had used it as the base for their training. To the north of Pen-y-Pass the road winds down the Llanberis Pass, between the huge rock buttresses which are the playgrounds of the modern rock climbers, to Llyn Peris and Llyn Padarn.

Llyn Peris has recently been drained and dammed to form the bottom lake of the huge Dinorwic Pump Storage Power Station. This hydro-electric scheme involves the use of two lakes, one high lake and one lower reservoir. The top lake, Marchlyn Mawr, behind Elidir Fawr to the north, stores the water until generating capacity is needed. The water is then released and drives the turbines built under the hillside opposite and flows into the lower lake, Llyn Peris. During off peak times the water is then pumped back to the higher lake for future use. It is a massive project involving deep underground workings and tunnels, well hidden in the slate quarries and underground, but visible across Llyn Peris. The electricity is fed into the national grid.

Llanberis, in the bottom of the valley, sits almost between the two lakes and is probably best known as the starting point for the Snowdon Mountain Railway. This is a rack and pinion railway carrying passengers to the summit; as an easy alternative to walking, it is very popular. Not far from the station is the Welsh Slate Museum, with exhibits and buildings relating to all aspects of quarry work. The old quarry railway has been rebuilt to provide a pleasant run along the North shore of Llyn Padarn through a country park of the same name. It is a narrow gauge railway, and many of the original locomotives are still in use.

To the north of the town and above the massive slate tips, rise the bulky slopes of Elidir Fawr and the Glyder range of mountains, most of which are over 3,000ft high. They are accessible on foot from the Llanberis side, but the most interesting walks and ascents are made from the north, starting mainly from Llyn Ogwen, where there are several convenient car parks. There is no village at Ogwen — just a collection of buildings comprising a youth hostel and an adventure school — but it is easy to get the feel of the high mountains despite the busy main road. The old packhorse road runs parallel to the modern road and can be traced for much of the distance along the valley side: the remains of the old packhorse bridge can be seen underneath the more modern road bridge by the falls below Llyn Ogwen.

Access to the mountains is by a footpath which climbs steeply from behind Ogwen Cottage, a Mountain Rescue Post, before levelling out into Cwm Idwal. The path then follows the shores of Llyn Idwal past the Idwal Slabs, perhaps some of the most frequently climbed rocks in the country. It climbs steeply to Twll Du or Devil's Kitchen, a narrow defile of black rock which seems to cut the mountain in half. The whole of Cwm Idwal is a nature reserve with many rare species of alpine plants and orchids found amongst the rocks. It was the early botanists who started the sport of rock climbing as they searched higher and higher for new specimens.

A pleasant afternoon can be enjoyed without leaving the cwm but the higher mountains, like Snowdon, are steep and rocky, though in many respects totally different from their neighbour.

Climbing on past Devil's Kitchen the path comes to a small lake (Llyn-y-Cwn) and then divides. To the right

M
2+h
*
ooo

Tryfan, Ogwen Valley

H
2-3h
****
ooo

the track climbs easily to the summit of Y Garn (3,104ft) then along the crest to Mynydd Perfedd and either west above Marchlyn Mawr, top lake of the pump storage scheme, to Elidir Fawr (3,029ft) or north to Carnedd-y-Filiast and down into Bethesda.

H
5+h
****
oooo

Taking the track on the left from Llyn-y-Cwn and going south east, the path rises steeply up the scree-covered slopes of Glyder Fawr (3,279ft) to the summit, a rather desolate boulder-strewn plateau. It continues along the ridge past the well-named Castle of the Winds to Glyder Fach (3,262ft) and the flat stone of cantilever, a perched block which seems delicately balanced but has so far defied all the efforts of large and small parties to dislodge it.

The views from both these summits are some of the finest in Snowdonia, looking down on the surrounding mountains and valleys, with the summit of Tryfan seemingly only a step away to the east. The path descends steeply alongside the Bristly Ridge to the cwm and then north back to Ogwen. However the summit of Tryfan (3,010ft), only a short scramble above, is well worth the extra effort for this is one of the true mountains of North Wales. With a sharp profile from every viewpoint it stands separated from all others above the valley. On this ascent one's hands will be needed for extra grip, as the path to the top is steep and rocky. The summit is crowned by two great monoliths, imaginatively known as Adam and Eve. They are close together and it is said that a true Welsh mountaineer is one who has stepped from one to the other. With the steep drop below it is safer not to attempt it, but to descend by the much slower, but safer, route back to the cwm, and then north down to Ogwen Cottage.

Old Pack Horse Bridge
below present bridge at
Ogwen Falls

Between the Nant Ffrancon Pass and Llyn Ogwen and the Conwy Valley is the largest range of hills, which rise steeply above the lake mainly north from Pen-yr-Oleu Wen (3,211ft) to Drum (2,529ft), then sloping more gently on the east to the foothills above Conwy. They are of a completely different character, being more rounded and grass-covered, with only occasional steep cliffs and cwms. The walking is more arduous and the route finding more difficult. As it is a large area with many access points, it is suggested that those considering mountain walking here should equip themselves with a large scale map and guide book to gain maximum enjoyment.

H
3h
****
ooo

Despite this advice, it would be unfair not to give at least a brief description of these hills. The main path ascends from the west end of Llyn Ogwen and rises very steeply for almost 2,000ft to the summit of Pen-yr-Oleu-Wen (3,211ft). Once this has been achieved, there is little further climbing for the whole length of the ridge. Circling round the very edge of one of the most perfect cwms, Ffynnon Lloer, the summit of Carnedd Dafydd (3,427ft) is soon reached; then on to Carnedd Llewelyn (3,458ft) From there a spur goes east providing

some interesting and mainly downhill walking, and for those who have had enough there is a circular return route to the valley. Going north from Carnedd Llewelyn, the ridge can be followed over Foel Grach (3,196ft), Foel Fras and then down to Drum (2,529ft). This would be a full day's excursion, and it is best to arrange transport at the northern end, if a long walk back is to be avoided.

H
7h
****
oooo

The smaller hills to the south of the main range are split by a series of deep valleys, each containing a lake of individual character dammed to provide water for industry in the Conwy Valley. The northernmost, Llyn Eigiau, burst its dam in 1925 causing a disastrous flood; the great masonry blocks and deep fissure created can be seen just below the remaining lake. The next, Llyn Cowlyd, is set in bleak uplands, while the two smaller ones to the south, Llyn Crafnant and Llyn Geirionydd, are in wooded valleys. The latter is a popular spot for day-trippers, yachtsmen and water skiers, though the roar of power boats upsets the serenity of this beautiful spot. All these valleys, with the exception of Cowlyd, can be reached easily by road from the Conwy Valley.

To the south is the Gwydyr Forest stretching from Llyn Crafnant to

Penmachno and covering many of the hills and valley sides. The forests have been developed since 1921 by the Forestry Commission and are now a Forest Park with free access. They are a fine introduction to the wilder mountains beyond.

There are many footpaths through the forest, some following long forgotten roads to old lead mines and quarries, while others follow delightful little streams to quiet mountain lakes — everybody is welcome provided that they respect the forest and natural environment. As the forest has many old copper and lead mines, care must be taken when walking near the shafts.

The small town of Betws-y-Coed is almost surrounded by the forest at the junction of three valleys, the Lledr Valley from the south, the Llugwy Valley from the east and the Conwy Valley to the north. It sits astride the A5 trunk road and is a frequent bottleneck in summer as most of the traffic has to cross the graceful Waterloo Bridge. There are hotels, cafes and a very large craft shop, while near the railway station is the Conwy Valley Railway Museum. The Tourist Information Centre has descriptive leaflets of the many short walks in the locality and in the nearby forest.

The main road rises through the town and just on the left is an old stone bridge with a small cataract below it — if you are lucky you may see salmon jumping. A few miles upstream and next to the road, are the Swallow Falls, a magnificent sight particularly after rainfall. The next village, Capel Curig, is merely a cross roads with a few climbing and other shops and several hotels. The imposing mountain across the lake is Moel Siabod; from this side it is one of the easier mountain walks. Start about one mile towards Betws-y-Coed at Pont Cyfyng where a small road turns off to a cluster of cottages. The main track begins there and follows an old quarry

H
3-4h
**
ooo

Waterloo Bridge

Swallow Falls near Betws-y-Coed

Places of Interest In and Around Betws-y-Coed

Waterloo Bridge
Built in the same year as the Battle of Waterloo, a superb cast iron bridge carrying the A5 over the river.

Conwy Valley Railway Museum
Housed in a purpose-built building adjacent to the station, with many items showing all aspects of railway life.

Swallow Falls
Good views of tumbling cataract just by the A5 above the village

Capel Garmon
Burial Chamber with remains of long barrow. North of A5 follow signs to Capel Garmon.

road which at first rises easily past the slate quarries and then follows the ridge with some easy scrambling to the grass slopes below the rocky summit cairn. There are fine views over the sheer drop to the cwm below. The path along and down the ridge to the Pen-y-Gwryd Hotel gives a long walk; it is best to return the way you came for the views are always different on the way back.

Just outside Capel Curig is Plas-y-Brenin, the National Mountaineering Centre, which provides courses in all grades of walking, climbing and skiing in the surrounding mountains, and canoeing on the nearby lake and river. The road then traverses a wide marshy valley with fine views of Snowdon, before descending from the Pen-y-Gwryd Hotel through the beautiful Nant Gwynant with its lake to Beddgelert. This gem of a village, perfectly situated at the entrance to the Aberglaslyn Pass, is a traffic bottleneck in summer.

The village thrives on the story of the legendary Gelert, a dog belonging to Prince Llewelyn which he slew after returning from a hunting trip on finding that his son was missing and the dog was covered in blood. It was only later that his son was found safe and a wolf dead nearby, obviously killed by the dog. He buried the faithful hound and the grave is just a short stroll alongside the river from the village centre. A similar story appears in other parts of the world, and it is most likely that it was introduced here by an over-zealous publican in the eighteenth century to encourage visitors. It is more probable that the Gelert referred to in the village name was an early Christian connected with a priory which once stood on that site.

Beddgelert is an ideal centre for exploring the surrounding hills, for

Beddgelert

Gelert's Grave

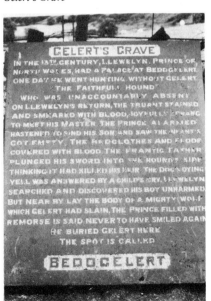

there are some fine hotels and guest houses: though a little crowded in summer, it has a charm of its own. The old Welsh Highland Railway passed close to the village. A pleasant stroll links up with this by following the signs from the village to Gelert's grave and continuing alongside the river banks to cross the old railway bridge and then along the railway (now disused) to Aberglaslyn. Then a series of tunnels brings one to Nantmor. For a long (about 9 miles), easy, but excellent walk one continues through Nantmor on the minor road, which traces the course of an old road to the junction. Turn left and follow that road past Cae Dafydd Potteries (with tea shop) along the valley with its bubbling stream to pass the slate quarries and descend to Nant Gwynant. A footpath can be followed along the banks of the river and around Llyn Dinas back to Beddgelert.

A variation on this route can be made after emerging from the long tunnel on the railway. Turn left here and follow a good footpath up Cwm

L
1-1½h
*
ooo

L
4h
*
oo

M
2+h
**
oooo

59

Bucket conveyor from copper mines near Aberglaslyn. Cwm Bychan

have been reclaimed and the river is impassable from Porthmadog.

The hills to the east of Aberglaslyn are fairly easily accessible on minor roads which branch off the main road from there to Penrhyndeudraeth. The first road up the Nantmor valley has several picnic spots and small parking areas; it is a beautiful area, but the road is narrow. From the high point on that road where there is an old slate quarry, a good little path opposite a white cottage goes up to Llyn Llagi. The path continues beyond the lake and over the shoulder to Llyn-yr-Adar and on the ridge of Cnicht. This can be traversed with wonderful views of the estuary and descended until the path breaks off to the right at a col below a small crag. It joins an old packhorse trail which, if followed to the right, goes downhill to the road following a lovely little stream back to the quarry. Several other footpaths leave this road for other lakes, and they are all fairly easy walking but as they may be damp underfoot, it is best to go well shod.

H
3+h
**
oooo

Cnicht, sometimes called the Matterhorn of North Wales, is best seen from the south, and with Moelwyn Bach and Moelwyn Mawr it stands proudly above the estuary. Croesor, a small village at the end of a minor road, is the best starting point for any walks on that range. The road to Croesor starts by a large gatehouse in Llanfrothen. It is narrow and high walled and passes Plas Brodanw, home of the late Sir Clough Williams-Ellis the architect, best known for the hotel and village of Portmeirion. Opposite the house a gate leads uphill to a small castle with superb views over the estuary; it is a 'folly', being the architect's wedding present from his brother officers during his time in the army. It is a short but very pleasant walk.

Bychan to some old mines and the remains of a bucket conveyor. The path then goes off to the left, across a small hollow, to the ridge above Nant Gwynant and then descends the old miners' track to a minor road and thence back to Beddgelert. There are many short and simple walks around the village. It is usually best to enquire locally about walks for the route very much depends on the time available.

South of Beddgelert, and downstream, is the well known Aberglaslyn Pass which must feature more often on calendars than any other place in Wales. It has all the components of a classic beauty spot. A steep sided valley, trees, a tumbling river and a bridge all combine perfectly and can be viewed with little effort from the roadside. At one time ships could sail right up to the bridge, but since the building of the embankment across the mouth of the estuary, the lands

Aberglaslyn Pass

Croesor Valley and Cnight

Small Castle near Llanfrothen

H
3h
**
ooo

From Croesor there is a well sign-posted track which follows the ridge to the top of Cnicht. It is an easy walk, with one difficult scrambling section just below the summit, but if care is taken it should present no problems.

H
3-4h
**
ooo

Moelwyn Mawr is best tackled by following the old quarry road beyond the village to the highest quarry, which until recently had a fine collection of buildings still surviving. From the back of the quarry the footpath up and over the shoulder brings one to the top, before descending down the ridge to the south and directly to the village.

Moelwyn Bach, the smaller of the two, can be approached from the south through a small forestry plantation at the high point of the road linking Croesor and Rhyd. The path is not too clear and it is wet underfoot, but once the ridge is reached walking is drier and straightforward: the views from the summit are magnificent; for ease it is suggested that the descent is made by the same route.

H
3h
**
ooo

There are many fine walks in this area and it is ideal for a good day out. There are also numerous abandoned quarries and slate mines to interest the industrial archaeologist. These hills are less frequented than those to the north, but there is still much to see and enjoy. But proper dress and equipment are essential.

5 Blaenau Ffestiniog, Barmouth and Bala

The area of country bounded on the north by the Lledr Valley and the Vale of Ffestiniog and to the south by Llyn Tegid and the Mawddach Estuary contains some of the best, and at the same time the least known, mountains of Snowdonia. The ranges to the north with fourteen peaks over 3,000ft are well known and well visited, but how many people are aware of the quieter slopes of the Rhinogs, the Arenigs and the surrounding hills?

Visitors to this area, either walking or touring, can expect some pleasant surprises. It is a large area crossed by few roads. The hills and moorlands are high, divided by long valleys bearing the inevitable main road; but the character of the country is such that there are few of these. On the side facing Tremadog Bay are 20 miles of beautiful golden sands with some of the best bathing in North Wales.

The towns in the area are small, reflecting much that is Welsh — not for them the bright lights and noise, but honest down-to-earth service, and the main language of the area is Welsh.

When the National Park was desig-

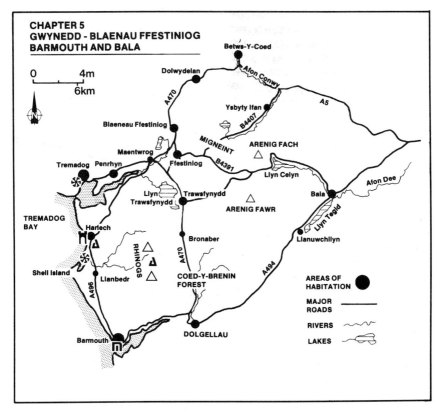

CHAPTER 5
GWYNEDD - BLAENAU FFESTINIOG
BARMOUTH AND BALA

nated, Blaenau Ffestiniog, almost in the centre, was excluded. As an industrial town, with huge slate tips towering above it, the grey terraces of houses blending in to give a gloomy view particularly in the rain, it was possibly considered to be a blot on the landscape. Now almost thirty years after that decision, the quarries no longer produce slate in any quantity and the once ugly town is ironically a popular centre for visitors. It is the slate they come to see, and slate artefacts they come to buy.

There are many sorts of mining and quarrying in North Wales, but it is slate for which the country is best known: until recently most buildings had a slate roof. Now with clay or concrete roof tiles, and even imitation slates, there is very little slate mined in the area. Several other towns have been dominated by slate, including Llanberis and Bethesda, but in Blaenau Ffestiniog everything is slate. It has

been the life and breath of the community for two hundred years, though now most of the quarries are quiet and the pumps switched off.

Slate underlies most of Snowdonia and appears frequently on or near the surface. Where it does appear it can be quarried, but around Blaenau it was found easier to mine it. Many of the seams are forty or fifty feet thick and tilted at an angle of 45 degrees; so the caverns created when the slate was removed are enormous.

Undoubtedly life in the quarry was hard: men usually all from the same family worked in small groups. They were paid according to their production, and there was no time for idling: they worked underground by candlelight. One man did the drilling to blast the rock loose, sometimes working high above the ground suspended only by a rope around one thigh. The others would break up and reduce the blocks to more manageable

The Ffestiniog Railway

sizes, ready for removal. Outside they would be shaped and dressed as required. Each size of roofing slate had its own name: countess, princess, wide lady and many more.

Two mines are open to the public in Blaenau Ffestiniog, on opposite sides of the A470 before it crosses the Crimea Pass to Dolwyddelan. On the north side is Gloddfa Ganol, the largest slate mine in the world, and on the south, the Llechwedd Slate Cavern; both have visitor centres and guided tours down the caverns to experience the miners' conditions. There are shops for souvenirs and one can watch slates being trimmed and cut in the old way. Justifiably, they are both very popular and can be well recommended.

For the walker it is possible to visit many of the older disused mines in the hills surrounding Blaenau though care must be taken and shafts avoided. A short distance from the town is Tanygrisiau, a small community surrounded by remnants of its slate-mining past and now the terminus of the Ffestiniog Railway. A steep track rises from the back of the village up to Llyn Cwmorthin and an old chapel; beyond are the barracks and sheds of the old quarries. The path uphill past the chapel continues to the old Rhosydd mines, the highest in Wales. It is easy to imagine the hardships of the miner as he walked this path to work at the beginning of each week. Here all the slate was mined, and the tunnels (or 'adits' as they are known) stretch up and through the hillside.

This is the back of Moelwyn Mawr and a walk up the old inclines or the old tracks through the Rhosydd quarry leads to two great holes from which the slate has been extracted. Just behind these and over the shoulder is a terraced track which can be followed easily around the hillside to

the south to above Llyn Stwlan, the top lake of a pump storage scheme. From there a road leads back downhill to Tanygrisiau and the station. The lower reservoir is a favourite place for trout fishermen. The adjacent power station can be visited by appointment, and there is a visitors' information centre, open daily during the season.

The Ffestiniog Railway, one of the great lines of Wales, runs between Blaenau Ffestiniog and Porthmadog. Operated now mainly by volunteers, this narrow gauge railway was originally built to carry the slate from the mines in Blaenau to the quay at Porthmadog. Now it provides a regular passenger service for most of the year. The scenery en route is superb, as the track drops from the hills down the beautiful Vale of Ffestiniog before skirting the estuary of Traeth Mawr and crossing the Cob (or embankment) to Porthmadog. It is more usual to catch the train at Porthmadog and do the return journey to and from the terminus near Blaenau Ffestiniog. The little engines are original and excellently maintained. A connecting

---

Places to Visit in the Vale of Ffestiniog

Plas Tan-y-Bwlch, Maentwrog, on A487.
Snowdonia National Park Centre, runs courses for visitors on countryside and aspects of the National Park.

Portmeirion
Beautiful Italianate village conceived by Sir Clough Williams-Ellis. Gardens, café and craft shops. Where *The Prisoner* was filmed. Off the A487 at Minfford.

bus runs up to the slate quarries for visitors.

Near neighbour to Blaenau Ffestiniog is Ffestiniog, a quiet little village, standing at the head of the valley to which it gives its name and with superb views of the surrounding mountains. Below, the Vale of Ffestiniog is justifiably said to be the most beautiful in North Wales. The steep sided slopes are covered in many places with the original oakwoods that once covered most of Wales. The Afon Dwyryd meanders lazily along the valley bottom to an ancient stone bridge at Maentwrog, a pleasant little village that takes its name from an old stone in the churchyard — Maen (stone) of Twrog. Now isolated from the sea, it was once a busy little port for the slate from the surrounding hills.

Across the valley is Plas Tan-y-Bwlch, the Snowdonia National Park Study Centre. Set in beautiful woodlands, the house once belonged to the wealthy Oakley family, owners of the quarries of Blaenau Ffestiniog. The centre runs many courses open to the public on all aspects of the countryside and the National Park. A nature trail starts from the car park by the house and wanders up through the woods to Llyn Mair, a small reservoir above, returning eastwards close to the railway and back to the garden. A second trail starts at the lake and circles through the woodland for about $\frac{3}{4}$ mile.

The lake, Llyn Mair (Mary's Lake), is an idyllic spot and can easily be approached by the steep road (B4410), past the Oakley Arms Hotel; there is a picnic area and car park and the rhododendrons are magnificent when in bloom. Just above is one of the stations for the Ffestiniog railway which curves and winds its way through the woods of Tan-y-Bwlch.

The river meanders slowly down to Penrhyndeudraeth where it is crossed by a toll bridge and then out to sea by Portmeirion. This small private village with its tiny harbour was designed and built by the late Sir Clough Williams-Ellis, the Welsh architect whose intention was to create a place free from careless building and adver-

Llyn Mair behind Tan-y-Bwlch in the Snowdonia National Park

Looking across from the hills to Harlech Castle and the Dunes

tising. The cottages, mainly in the Italian style, are grouped around a small bay and contain many features collected from other buildings and saved for posterity. The hotel, the centrepiece of the village, was sadly destroyed by fire in 1981, and, with it, many of Sir Clough's drawings and records. The village has craft shops and restaurants, and many of the cottages are available for rental. It is on a private estate but visitors are welcome, though charged; access is off the A487 at Minfford.

Across the sandy estuary from Portmeirion the hills rise steeply to the lofty summits of the Rhinog Range. It is a delightful range of hills stretching twenty miles to the south, dotted here and there with little lakes and woodlands, penetrated, but never crossed, by single-track mountain roads. It follows the magnificent

Places of Interest Around Blaenau Ffestiniog

Llechwedd Slate Caverns
Trips inside the slate caverns ty tram, and to the deeper caverns by special railway. Demonstrations of slate working and photos of life in quarries. Slide and photographic displays.

Glodfa Ganol
Displays of massive machinery of slate industry and visits to the mines wearing helmets and miners' lamps. Collection of old steam engines.

Ffestiniog Power Station
First pumped storage scheme in Britain. Tours of the power station and the top lake are available. Book at the information centre at Tanygrisiau

sweep of the bay right down to Barmouth.

At the northern end of the range the coastal land of Morfa Harlech is wide, backed by huge sand dunes from which the sea has retreated. The town of Harlech stands pinched between the sea and the hills with the castle perched high on a rocky outcrop dominating the surrounding area.

Built by Edward I in 1238 on the very edge of the bay the castle must have served as a strong reminder to the Welsh of the power of the king, for it is visible for many miles around. The sea has now retreated, but it is nevertheless striking. It came under attack many times from the Welsh before being taken in 1404 by Owain Glyndwr. It served for some time as his capital before being re-taken by the English in 1408. During the Wars of the Roses the Lancastrians held out there for eight years before fleeing overseas. One survivor, a 12-year-old boy, went on to become Henry VII,

and it is said that this siege inspired the march *Men of Harlech*. It was the last Welsh fortress to be captured during the Civil War, but since then has been left to become a ruin, a grand ruin however, with an inner courtyard surrounded by two mighty walls surmounted by narrow walkways. There are magnificent views over the estuary, the mountains to the north and the Lleyn Peninsula. The castle is best approached from the town side to gain a full appreciation of the difficulties faced by an attacker.

A short distance to the south of the town in the fields above the road is Muriaur Gwyddelod or Irishman's Walls, believed to have been built by settlers from Ireland between 1,000 and 2,000 years ago. The walls are a circular enclosure about 4ft high and subdivided into 'rooms'; there are several similarly named sites in North Wales, but we can only guess their true origin.

The beaches along the bay below

Llandanwg Church on the Dunes

Places of Interest Near Harlech

Harlech Castle
Fine castle in superb situation. Scene of many bloody battles and inspiration for the march *Men of Harlech.*

Muriaur Gwyddelod, Irishmans Walls
Situated in fields south of Harlech. Remains of early Iron Age settlements possibly Irish.

Llanfair Slate Caverns
Walk in caverns of old slate mine and see the real conditions. 2 miles south of Harlech on A496.

Beaches
The whole of the bay in front of Harlech has beautiful golden sands with lots of room for everyone.

Harlech are some of the finest; they are backed by sand dunes and are wide enough for the most energetic game of football. Stretching from Harlech Point in the north almost to Barmouth in the south, they are safe for bathing and never crowded. Access to the beaches is from the A496 and is signposted. The Royal St David's golf course lies behind the dunes.

South of Harlech at Llandanwg (there is a car park right behind the dunes), an interesting medieval church lies buried by sand nearby. At Llanbedr the road to Shell Island is directly opposite the Youth Hostel and goes across a causeway which is covered at high tide. There is a charge to reach the island for day visitors, but, as may be guessed, it is a great spot to collect shells and enjoy the sea. Also in Llanbedr is the recently opened Maes

Artro, a commune of craftsmen and artists making everything from candles to gems. It is an imaginative scheme giving an opportunity to visitors to see many local craftsmen at work. There is a playground for children, an aquarium with specimens of locally found fish, and a restaurant, all pleasantly laid out in a small area of woodland.

It is thought that in prehistoric times this particular section of the coastline was the main landing spot for trade with Ireland. There are many old tracks and roadways leading into and across the hills from Llandanwg and Llanbedr. Several tracks can be traced continuously into England. Many of the old tracks, now metalled roads, into the hills, are steep and narrow but lead to some fascinating places.

One such road leaving Llanbedr beside the Victoria Hotel divides after 1½ miles. The right fork goes up to Cwm Nantcol, a beautiful isolated valley below Rhinog Fach and Rhinog Fawr and a good spot from which to ascend these mountains. The left fork follows the narrow wooded valley of the Afon Artro to the head of Cwm Bychan, where there is a parking spot by the lake; from here the famous Roman Steps can be followed, The footpath leads across the stream and through the woods to the start of the Steps which lead over the shoulder of Rhinog Fawr before descending to the valley beyond. The steps are an interesting walk, particularly if at the highest point you turn left and walk into the hills to the north; the rock scenery is superb, with huge perched rocks (glacial erratics) sometimes the size of small houses deposited on the glacier-polished granite. The Steps are man-made, but there is no evidence that they are Roman. It is more likely that they were a medieval pack-

M
1-3h
*
oooo

Reproduction Welsh village in Maes Artro

point, with magnificent views over Harlech, the estuary and the Lleyn Peninsula beyond. The tarmac road then dips down to the left around the hillside but directly in front is a rocky track, leading first to an Iron Age hill fort that crowns the hill, and then continuing north into and across this range of mountains. There is a possibility that at one time this track was the main road to England from the coast and Ireland, for, though overgrown now, it is terraced into the hillside and paved across the marshes. There are many hut circles and standing stones along the route indicating its importance. If time allows, it makes a good (fairly easy) walk.

The tarmac road which can be followed more easily runs at a high level parallel with the coast for about five miles to a small lake. From here a road to the left drops steeply down to rejoin the coast road; or it is possible to continue on this minor road for several more miles and return by the same route. This is a splendid drive

horse trail, though the route could very easily be the same as an earlier prehistoric track which can be traced and followed right through the hills to Bala.

Perhaps the finest road into the hills leaves the coast road from the village of Llanfair. It climbs easily for a mile or two, with several large standing stones beside the road, to the highest

---

Places of Interest Around Llanbedr

Llandanwg Church
Ancient church on beach nearly buried by sand dunes. Signposted from A496.

Shell Island
Connected by causeway, covered at high tide. Sand dunes and excellent beach with café and bars. Millions of shells to collect. Turn off A496 in Llanbedr opposite the Youth Hostel.

Roman Steps
At head of Cwm Bychan, footpath leads from lake to the steps. Remains of ancient packhorse trail with well preserved steps. Picnic spot at lakeside. Turn off at Victoria Hotel in Llanbedr.

Maes Artro
Village containing workshops of craftsmen including weavers, potters, clockmakers and gold and silversmiths plus many more. You can watch them at work and buy if you wish. Aquaria, playgrounds and cafés, something for everyone. Adjacent to A496 just south of Llanbedr.

Places of Interest Around Barmouth and the Mawdach Estuary

RNLI Maritime Museum on quay in Barmouth
Lifeboat and other ship models, old photographs.

Barmouth Estuary
Footpath across the railway bridge over the estuary gives good views of the estuary and Cader Idris to the south.

Old Country Life Centre, off A496 at Taly-y-bont.
Glimpses of bygone days in the country with traditional tools, crafts, fashions and other aspects. Old mill now houses restaurant and gift shop.

Weaver's Loft Jubilee Road, Barmouth
Weaving shop producing tapestries and tweed.

Coed-y-Brenin Forest and Visitor Centre
Displays of Forestry Machinery and Methods. Plus many tracks of interest in the forest and environs. Turn off A470 at Pont Dolgefeiliau.

Rhaeadr Mawddach and Pistyll Cain
In the forest to the east, follow the footpath from the picnic spot at Pont Dolgefeiliau. Map obtainable at visitor centre as above.

M,H
**
oooo

though care must be taken as the road is single track with few passing places; it can be joined at several points by climbing steeply from the coast road.

Further down the coast there are other pre-historic remains fairly close to the road particularly in the Dyffryn Ardudwy area. There is a fine old drovers' road crossing the hills almost to Dolgellau. In the Rhinog range of hills there are, in fact, so many old roadways and trackways for the walker to explore that, armed with an Ordnance Survey map, he can be sure of an excellent day's walking simply by following any of them. He can have the hills virtually to himself all day long, with some of the finest, and on occasions the most unusual, scenery in North Wales.

The main seaside resort along this coast is Barmouth, squeezed tightly between the hills and the sea. It owes much of its popularity to the railway and the Victorian penchant for sea bathing, much of the architecture reflecting that era. The railway still plays an important part in the life of Barmouth, for the railway bridge across the estuary is falling into a state of disrepair and is in danger of being permanently closed. This would split the whole stretch of trackway from Aberdovey in the south to Pwllheli on the Lleyn Peninsula. It is a superb train journey following the narrow coastal belt between the sea and hills and crossing many estuaries with outstanding views of the mountains inland. Every effort should be made to keep the bridge and complete line open, as much as a service for local people as for visitors.

Today Barmouth is still a popular town in a beautiful setting; it has some fine beaches and whether approached by sea, road or rail, the scenery is breathtaking. The estuary of the Afon Mawddach is similar to a Norwegian fjord with its steeply wooded slopes and surrounding mountains. The road (A496) from Dolgellau, clinging in many places to the very edges of the shore, is particularly scenic with views across to Cader Idris high above the opposite bank.

At the head of the estuary is the very Welsh market town of Dolgellau, a compact little town with narrow streets that seems to be the dividing line between North and Mid Wales. Despite its position and its sixteenth-century bridge, its has figured little in Welsh history, the area to the south being commanded by the mighty summit of Cader Idris (2,927ft). It is a good centre for exploring the surrounding hills and valleys with a number of easy walks in the locality, details of which are available from the Tourist Information Centre.

We shall head north again, along the Afon Mawddach upstream from Llanelltyd and through the Coed-y-Brenin Forest, where the valley is narrow and the river tumbles steeply over rocks and waterfalls. It is to the hillsides around this river that the prospectors came, and still come, in search of gold and other minerals. Mining is only on a small scale though many optimists still believe that there is much gold to be found. The main workings are around the waterfalls of Pistyll Cain and Rhaeadr Mawddach on the upper reaches of the river. Gold mining has been sporadic, but there has been the recent disturbing trend of multi-national mining companies making trial bores to investigate the possibility of tapping the numerous resources in and around the valley. There are occasional rumours of great belts of copper lying beneath the valleys of Snowdonia but so far the conservationists have been successful in blocking all attempts at large scale mining.

The Coed-y-Brenin Forest covers approximately 16,000 acres in the main and outlying valleys, and it spreads high on the slopes almost to Rhinog Fach and Rhinog Fawr. The Forestry Commission's Visitors' Centre, just off the A470 at the bridge of Pont Dolgefeiliau, gives an excellent introduction to many aspects of forestry, past and present; it also has a display of gold mining machinery, There are many footpaths and forest roads in the main and upper valleys of the forest, and a map is obtainable at the centre clearly describing many of the tracks, including the popular walks to the waterfalls and gold mines.

The road (A470) continues north through the forest and on to the high moorlands, a straight and easy drive allowing plenty of time to enjoy the views before reaching the village of Trawsfynydd. The village has achieved dubious fame by being the site of the first inland nuclear power station. Standing on the shores of the nearby lake, the large square structure seems

Tomen-y-Mur Roman Fort near Trawsfynydd

to fit well into the scenery, in many ways enhancing the nearby hills.

A short distance beyond the power station a small road goes off to the right under a railway bridge and between steep banks to a wood. Here by a gate are the mounds of a small Roman Amphitheatre, unique in Wales. It was part of the camp of Tomen-y-Mur, visible as a small mound across the field. It must have been an isolated posting for a legionary born and bred on the Mediterranean coast, especially when the north westerlies blew in the winter. Nevertheless it was in a fine position and perhaps he could take comfort from the beauty of the surrounding hills.

The main road now drops sharply into the Vale of Ffestiniog from which we started, or turns right through Ffestiniog and Blaenau Ffestiniog to cross the Crimea Pass. The descent into the Lledr Valley is steep, but gives some splendid views of the southern slopes of Moel Siabod. We pass through Roman Bridge, which has no Roman connections, to Dolwyddelan and its small castle. Built about 1170 as the home of Llewelyn the Great, the castle has several interesting features, but is small compared with Edward's fortresses on the coast.

The road winds through the Gwydyr Forest to meet and cross the River Conwy close to Betws-y-Coed. A short distance upstream from the bridge is the Fairy Glen and Conwy Falls, easily approached by a pleasant path along the river bank. Above the falls, the river divides into the Afon Machno which turns south west along the lovely Cwm Penmachno. The River Conwy continues up the valley for several more miles before turning south west near Pentrefoelas.

Leaving the busy main road (A5) the Conwy turns towards its source, followed closely by a minor road. Halfway up the valley is the community of Yspytty Ifan. It was a hospice run by the Knights of St John for the pilgrims on their way to Bardsey Island, but there are now few traces of its past. Four miles to the south is Llyn Conwy, source of this famous river. The surrounding moorland was until the Dissolution a sanctuary and, despite the many passing pilgrims, was known for its lawlessness. Today the area is equally notorious; known as the Migneint it is a marshy plateau with few tracks, crossed only the by the roads from Yspytty Ifan and Penmachno. Close to the junction is an old decorated well which probably has associations with the old pilgrims.

To the south stand the two peaks of Arenig Fawr and Arenig Fach. The taller, Arenig Fawr, stands to the south of its smaller sister, separated by a road, stream and railway. The now disused railway was the main line from Ffestiniog and Bala to England. Running high above Cym Prysor from Trawsfynydd and crossing a high viaduct which now seems quite out of place in these wild moorlands; it was a magnificent journey under full steam. The Afon Tryweryn stream runs towards Bala but was dammed early in the 1960s to form Llyn Celyn which now supplies water to Liverpool. Beneath the waters of the lake was the small community of Capel Celyn, mainly a Quaker village, from where many families left to settle in America with the Pilgrim Fathers. A small chapel and carved rock on the northern shore commemorate the village. Below the dam the river is used for international canoe races, the water level being controlled from the reservoir; it joins the River Dee at Bala.

The town of Bala was famous before the Industrial Revolution for its woollen stockings, but has little other history of note. It takes its name from the Welsh 'bala' meaning outlet, for there the Dee starts its journey to the sea from the nearby lake. Despite its central position in Wales, at the junction of many old roads, Edward I seems to have found it strategically unimportant. There is a small mound or motte in the town believed to be of Norman origin though there are doubts even about that.

It is a grey stone town with a wide

Memorial Stone to the Quaker Village at Llyn Celyn

main street and was for many years the home of the Rev Thomas Charles (1755-1814), founder of the British and Foreign Bible Society and a pioneer of Methodism in North Wales; his statue stands in the main street. It continued as a Methodist stronghold when the Rev Lewis Edwards started an academy in 1837 on the outskirts of the town for young Methodist ministers. Many other Methodists left the town to start a colony in Patagonia in 1865, founding the town of Trelew where the families still live and farm, using Welsh as their first language.

Modern Bala is something of a holiday centre, reflecting little of its Methodist upbringing. It stands at the head of Llyn Tegid or Bala Lake, the largest natural lake in Wales, a favourite spot for yachtsmen as the occasional strong south-westerly wind can give exhilirating sailing. Known also for the fishing, both fly and coarse, the lake yields a unique species called the gwyniad believed to be a survivor from the ice age. It is a small fish resembling a herring that spurns the rod and is only occasionally caught by net. There are several specimens in the White Lion Hotel in the town.

The roads on each side of the lake make this shore line accessible for most of its length, with several pleasant picnic and parking areas off the minor road to the south. A recent addition along the southern bank is the Bala Lake Railway, a narrow gauge railway following the old main line which has steam and diesel engines running the full length of the lake. The main station is at Llanuwchllyn at the south end of the lake.

On the northern side of Llyn Tegid the main road A494 speeds between Bala and Barmouth, but for those with more time several metalled tracks across the hills towards Trawsfynydd provide an interesting and adventurous trip. Starting from Llanuwchllyn the recommended route follows the course of the Afon Lliw over to Bronaber and Trawsfynydd. Two miles up the left-hand side above the road is Castell Carndochan, possibly a Norman motte, but more likely the home of an unknown brigand. Nearby are the characteristic white spoil heaps from a nineteenth century gold mine. The road climbs steeply into the very heart of the mountains following the course of an ancient highway before descending through the forests to Bronaber on the Trawsfynydd to Dolgellau road.

It is a wild mountain road passing through some beautiful countryside and forests. Walkers should be armed with the necessary Ordnance Survey maps, either sheet 124 or 125, and a compass. There are few tracks and fewer walkers, and one must be prepared. Please remember also that, though all the hills and countryside are within the Snowdonia National Park, most of the land is privately owned. Walls and fences should not be damaged.

H
all day
***
ooo

6 The Lleyn Peninsula

There is much to commend the Lleyn Peninsula to either the casual visitor or longer-stay holiday maker. Stretching for 30 miles into the Irish Sea it is a land of superb scenery and fine beaches equal to any coastline in Europe. In recent years it has seen a vast growth in its summer population, but, despite this it has retained its Welsh charm and language; it is easy to imagine that one is in a different country. Divided from the bulk of Snowdonia by a range of hills of grand stature but of limited height, it has something for everyone. With innumerable beaches, bays and coves, it provides for the boating enthusiast and the bather. There are cliffs for the climber, golf courses and enough open spaces and sea cliffs to keep bird watchers, botanists and casual ramblers happy.

For convenience we shall regard the Caernarfon-Beddgelert-Porthmadog road as the eastern boundary of the area. The hills dividing the Snowdon Massif from the Lleyn border the

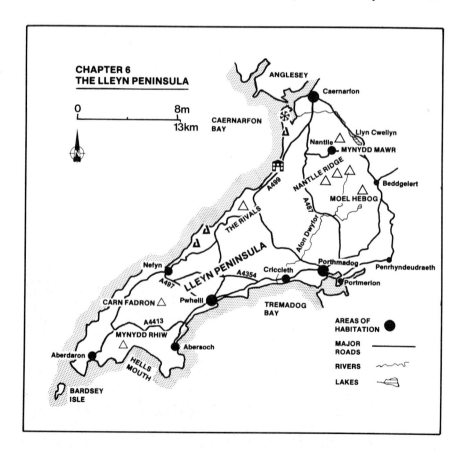

road to the west. Shortly after leaving Caernarfon the first great lump of Mynydd Mawr (2,291ft) can be seen as it stands sentinel, like a huge elephant, at the head of the valley. Below it is Llyn Cwellyn and the famous Snowdon Ranger Youth Hostel. It is a good walk to the summit for those prepared for lots of effort and little excitement. The approach is from the top of the pass on the Rhyd-Ddu to Nantlle road just after a small lake.

In past literature the little lake known as Llyn-y-Dywarchen has achieved more fame than Snowdon itself. It had a legendary floating island visited and confirmed by many early travellers to Wales, and was once considered as one of the Wonders of Wales. Today there is no evidence of such an island and we shall never again see cows floating across the lake on it.

From the top of the pass, a rather gloomy place, the view to the west is one of slate waste an huge tips. What devastation man has created in the pursuit of money! Around the village of Nantlle many of these huge craters have now filled with water, but efforts are being made to restore the machinery and workings of one mine above the village.

On the mountain, the path leaves from the top of the pass and is followed from the western end of the lake near a small building. It rises easily at first through a miniature rocky pass up an easy grass slope until it narrows towards the summit with views straight down to Llyn Cwellyn. The descent is by the same route.

H
3h
**
oo

To the south of the pass rises Y Garn, a spur of Mynydd Drws-y-Coed, the northernmost peak of the Nantlle ridge. The traverse of the

H
all day
***
oooo

Llyn Dinas looking towards Beddgelert, Moel Hebog in cloud on the left, Yr Aran's conical shape to the right

ridge is an excellent day's walking, covering in all five peaks over 2,000ft. The route is not difficult to follow with the aid of a good map and compass, but for many it will be a major expedition and is outside the scope of this guide.

South from Rhyd-Ddu stretches the Beddgelert Forest, covering much of the lower slopes of Moel Hebog. The Forestry Commission has done much to encourage people to use the forest; there is an excellent camp site and caravan site, a visitor information centre and shop. Available at the shop is an orienteering map of the forest — for those who have never tried the sport, it is an excellent introduction and a good way to spend the afternoon, testing their navigational skills, and exploring the forest, but old clothes are essential.

L
½-3h
*
ooo

From the car park in the forest starts one of several paths leading up Moel Hebog (2,566ft). It is one of the friendliest mountains in the area, with certainly some of the finest views. The path is clear for most of the way, following the stream right up through the forest, until breaking clear just below a small crag on the left. Halfway up the crag, and reached by a tricky scramble is Ogof (cave of) Owain Glyndwr. Overlooking the valley it is reputed to be the hide-out of the Welsh fourteenth century leader but is so small and damp that it hardly befits the hero's grandeur. On the same crag, but much easier to reach, is a small hollow in the cliff, which is a disused asbestos mine, though the narrow seam must have proved uneconomic.

H
3-5h
**
oooo

The path continues more steeply now to the col, and at a wall one turns left for Moel Hebog and right for Moel Lefn (2,094ft), a minor summit that is worth climbing. The summit of Moel Hebog is reached after a steep climb alongside the wall. The views are magnificent: to the north lies the Nantlle ridge; to the east the Snowdon Range and in the distance Moel Siabod, Cnicht and the Moelwyns: south are the Rhinogs and Tremadog Bay; while to the west the Lleyn Peninsula is at one's feet and on a clear day the coast of Ireland can be seen.

One can descend by the same route but it is better to return eastwards down the path to Cwm Cloch farm and Beddgelert and then walk about a

*Porthmadog with Cnicht
and the Meolwyns behind*

H
2-3h
*
ooo

mile back to the forest. The route is equally enjoyable if started from Beddgelert, where the path starts just out on the road to Rhyd-Ddu. Cross the river and go up the lane to a farm at Cwm Cloch. A signpost on the end of the barn directs one up the path which rises easily at first but becomes more steep near the summit.

South of Moel Hebog the lower hills give some pleasant rambling: but as paths are scarce one has to pick one's route carefully. All give excellent views particularly over the reclaimed estuary of Traeth Mawr to the south. The estuary of the Afon Glaslyn, known as Traeth Mawr, was once said to be the most beautiful in the whole of Wales. It is now about 7,000 acres of reclaimed land, and is frequently flooded after heavy rain. It was created by the building of the Embankment (the Cob) across its mouth in 1808 by William Madocks MP. At one time the estuary was navigable up the Aberglaslyn Bridge. Madocks's intention was to create an easy crossing point for traffic to the Lleyn Peninsula in order to open it up for the Irish trade. He also hoped to dry out the enclosed land for farming. His first intention never succeeded, the second has to a certain extent, providing grazing land only.

Madocks built the village of Tremadog, and later Porthmadog to be the port for his great plans. Both names have been converted recently

81

to the Welsh: so apart from a statue in Porthmadog little evidence remains of his influence on the project. He lived at Tan-yr-Allt above Tremadog and the village was laid out to please him. The poet Shelley was a frequent guest at the house and T. E. Lawrence (Lawrence of Arabia) was born in the village. The village is still of interest to architects and builders, its stone houses neatly built on each side of a square. Below the cliffs what looks like a town hall was in fact a theatre with access from the adjoining hotel on one side, with the cottage at the other end as the changing rooms; it is now a craft shop.

Behind the village, though hidden from the road by woodlands, and stretching for about one mile are Tremadog Rocks. They are a favourite area for rock climbing, particularly if it is raining further inland. The woods at the bottom are a nature reserve, much of it being natural growth with native trees.

Porthmadog was originally planned to be the lesser of the two towns but grew to pre-eminence with the opening of the port and the construction of the railway from Ffestiniog across the Cob. Slates were exported direct from the mines, but the trade died when the mines were closed, so that even the old slate sheds have gone — now replaced by holiday flatlets on the quayside. The railway is still running as the famous Ffestiniog Railway, with its terminus on the quayside.

The port has now been taken over by yachtsmen, but because of the silting of the estuary they must choose their sailing times by the tide. Until recent years it was a pleasant little harbour to stroll around, but there is now little of interest, though with the opening of a Maritime Museum on an original sailing ship, efforts are being made to revitalise it. The town has a pleasant shopping centre with many

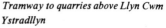

Tramway to quarries above Llyn Cwm Ystradllyn

Cwm Ystradllyn Slate Mill

Welsh craft shops to entice the visitor, and a pottery on the outskirts of the town where all are welcome to try their hand.

Several beaches are easily reached from the town centre; the nearest just around the headland is Borth-y-Gest, which has fine golden sands and small coves, but bathing is not too safe as the estuary is tidal. Next to it is Morfa Bychan or Black Rock Sands, much safer for bathing but more dangerous for walking. This is a two-mile stretch of wide flat beach backed by a large caravan site; parking is allowed on the beach.

L
½-2h
*
ooo

Behind is the grand little hill of Moel-y-Gest, which is a pleasant little viewpoint from which to survey the coast. There are several signposted footpaths which take no more than half an hour to the summit.

Inland from the coast are several minor roads leaving the main Caernarfon road (A4085) about two miles outside Tremadog. The first goes up to Cwm Ystradllyn past the magnificent ruin of a slate mill and then up to a reservoir. Parking is possible at the end of the road, and the hill in front is an easier alternative route to the summit of Moel Hebog. The peaceful valley may be explored by following the unmetalled road. The retaining wall below the slate tip has a superb curve.

H
2h
**
ooo

The road to the north passes Brynkir Woollen Mills (open to the public) where Welsh tapestries, flannels and tweeds are woven, and continues up to Cwm Pennant. This is a beautiful little valley as it winds right into the hills with lots of tumbling streams and places to walk or picnic. It is also possible to reach this valley by turning off the main road at Dolbenmaen just past the castle mound.

Criccieth, the next town along the coast, is a popular resort with several good beaches; the one immediately in front of the town is a good place to launch a dinghy or swim. Above the harbour is the only major castle on the

Retaining wall above the old tramway at
Cwm Ystradllyn

Old slate quarry at Cwm Ystradllyn near
Porthmadog

Llyn Gwynant from near A498 south east of Pen-y-Pass

Lleyn and though little remains but the gateway it looks impressive from any angle. It is not one of Edward I's castles, being merely enlarged by him on the site of an earlier Welsh castle. From the castle the views are magnificent and with the well developed hotel trade it is an excellent centre for touring the peninsula and mountains. Lloyd George, the statesman and Prime Minister, knew Criccieth well, for he spent his childhood in Llanystumdwy, just two miles away. He was educated in the village and died at Ty Newydd, a house he owned above the Criccieth road. His grave, designed by Sir Clough Williams-Ellis, is beside the river close to the bridge. There is a small museum with many mementoes of him in the village.

Shortly after Llanystumdwy, the road divides, that to the north providing a fast route across the Lleyn to Nefyn, while the main road continues to amble down the coast. About one mile after passing a holiday camp (day visitors are allowed), a small signpost directs one to Penarth Fawr, an interesting and attractive fifteenth-century manor house. Consisting basically of one room, it is well preserved and generally fairly quiet.

Pwllheli, the administrative centre and largest town, is perhaps the capital of the Lleyn. It has little of historical interest, but with its shops and beaches it is a popular centre for holidaymakers. The town and beach are separated by about half a mile and several centuries, the town being typically old Welsh and the houses along the promenade being a mixture of typical Victorian and modern. The harbour, protected by a hook of land which almost encloses it, is safe and, with Gimlet Rock at its entrance, easy to find.

The sand and shingle beaches face south and stretch for almost five miles to Llanbedrog and its rocky point.

Grave of Lloyd George beside the river at Llanstumdwy

The bathing is excellent along the whole coastline and once round the headland the beaches continue for several more miles along St Tudwal's Bay.

Abersoch is a favourite spot and the small town is now surrounded by caravan sites and holiday homes. It is a delightful little village with a small harbour, that has developed in the last 20-30 years as the centre for boating enthusiasts in North Wales. With two sheltered bays and wide safe beaches it is ideal for launching and sailing boats of all sizes.

Just off the coast are two small islands, no longer inhabited, known as St Tudwal's Islands, after the saint who founded a chapel there in the sixth century. Little remains of its Augustinian priory, and the islands are left to the birds and the lighthouse. Boat trips can be taken around the islands, thus also giving the opportunity to view the superb coastline from the sea.

Sailing near Criccieth

Nearing the end of the Lleyn the villages seem to get smaller and more widely scattered. Llangian, near Abersoch, is of some interest as one of the best kept villages in the county and for the sixth century stone in the churchyard carved in Latin commemorating Melus, the first mention of a doctor in Wales.

Crossing behind the long bay of Porth Neigwl or Hell's Mouth, the road climbs steeply over the shoulder of Mynydd Rhiw. This is a small hill criss-crossed by tracks and almost surrounded by roads, and, 999ft high, it has some pleasant walks with excellent views of the coastline. Early man may have appreciated the hill for the same reason, for there are several archaeological sites to be found on the hillside, including at the northern end a Stone Age axe factory. Towards Aberdaron the scenery is superb but somewhat marred by what seems like a forest of telegraph and electricity poles and their overhead lines.

Aberdaron is a tiny village on the very edge of the sea, the last stop for the pilgrims on their way to Bardsey Island. A café and a souvenir shop, Y Gegin Fawr, the Big Kitchen, was formerly a hostel and resting place before the crossing, while a small church on the very edge of the shore served their spiritual needs on the last lap.

Abersoch moorings

Abersoch with St Tudwals Island behind

Beaches on the South Coast of the Lleyn Peninsula

Near Porthmadog
Borth-y-Gest: Small bays and coves and tidal estuary.
Black Rock Sands: Two miles of good wide sands, saft bathing, drive your car onto the beach. Very popular and backed by caravan sites.

Near Criccieth
Two fine beaches divided by castle, safe bathing and launching facilities for small boats.

Llanbedrog
Sandy bay sheltered by headland. Ideal for bathing, boating, fishing and walks on headland.

Abersoch
Popular seaside resort with miles of fine golden sands. Very popular but still quite charming. Yacht club and mooring facilities, a sailor's paradise.

Porth Neigwl, Hell's Mouth
Open sandy beach about 4 miles long, plenty of room for everybody.

Aberdaron
Good beach with safe bathing and boating, last stop for the pilgrims on the way to Bardsey Island. Interesting old church on the edge of the beach. Good headland walks.

*Looking toward the end of the Lleyn
Peninsula and Bardsey Island*

Bardsey Island had various names in Welsh, but Ynys Enlli, or Island of Currents, as many a sailor and pilgrim will testify, is the most appropriate. Bardsey, (a Norse name) has been a place of pilgrimage since the sixth century, becoming so popular that many of the Welsh Bishops had their bodies transported and buried there. Little remains of the priory and the later flourishing community, but it is still a place surrounded by myths, mists and legends. Now it is an important centre for the study of birds and is owned by the Bardsey Island Trust.

The headland opposite Bardsey Island is a fine windswept spot, owned by the National Trust. It is a superb place to appreciate the beauty and setting of the Island with only the birds for company.

L
*
ooo

Northwards the cliff scenery is magnificent and there are many fine walks, broken only by the fine coves of Porth Oer and Porth Colmon. The former is more commonly known as Whistling Sands for the remarkable little squeak given off as one walks on it or runs one's hands through the sand. Apparently the quartz content of the sand is rounded and of uniform size, and when moved, produces a note of uniform pitch.

From this section of coast the most obvious feature when looking inland is the conical hill which thrusts its way upwards. This is Carn Fadron (1,217 ft) equidistant between the north and south shores, and the views from its summit are excellent. The hill has innumerable ancient trackways with much evidence of Iron Age settlement, and its exploration provides a pleasant alternative to lounging on the beach.

L
½-2h
**
ooo

Nefyn and Morfa Nefyn are perhaps the most popular holiday centres along this coast. They both have fine sheltered beaches, ideal for boating and bathing, and, like most of the

Porthdinllaen, the village on the beach

beaches on the peninsula, have superb views of the mountains, in this case Yr Eifl or the Rivals. Lacking pleasure parks and sideshows, they are ideal for quiet family holidays, with many guest houses and hotels in the villages and caravan sites in the environs.

Nefyn is the larger of the two and was once a major resting point for the pilgrims to Bardsey Island. Porth Dinllaen is a fine natural harbour and its small community can be reached only by a walk along the beach or across the golf course from Morfa Nefyn. It is a delightful collection of beach cottages, mostly holiday homes. A gentle stroll at low level around the headland takes one to the lifeboat station and a small sandy beach.

Nefyn, and more particularly Porth Dinllaen, was suggested during the early nineteenth century as an alternative to Holyhead as the major port to Ireland. The defeat of the motion by one vote in Parliament, saved this beautiful stretch of coast for all to enjoy. North along the beach from Nefyn is Bird rock, a craggy headland appropriately named for the many different species found there.

Towering above this stretch of coastland and visible from almost anywhere on Lleyn is Yr Eifl, anglicised to 'The Rivals' but meaning The Forks, because of the three peaks. The highest (1,849ft) is flanked on the seaward side by a much quarried summit (1,458ft), and on the inland side by the third peak (1,591ft), surmounted by the ruins of the Iron Age hillfort village of Tre'r Ceiri. This site, reached by a steep path from a stile on the Llanaelhaearn road, has the best preserved and most extensive collection of walled huts in the country. What a superb situation for a village. The site covers about five acres of the hill top. Surrounded by several defensive walls, (the inner one still with much of its parapet), it contains the remains of about fifty huts. Though never properly excavated, and unfortunately not

Defensive walling of the Iron Age hillfort of Tre'r Ceiri

Beaches on the Northern Side of Lleyn

Whistling Sands (Porth Oer)
Beautiful bay with safe bathing and unique sands that whistle as you walk across them.

Porth Iago
Approached along farm track. Delightful cove, worth finding, a good day out for the whole family.

Porth Colmon, Penllech Beach
Long stretch of sand with cliff and rock walks, caves, fishing and good bathing. Interesting church in the village of Llangwynadl.

Tudweiliog
Pleasant beach with fine sands, fairly small but private. Lovely walks along the coast.

Edern
Safe bathing, good fishing and boats for hire, power and row boats.

Nefyn and Morfa Nefyn
Excellent beaches on wide sandy bays. Popular resorts for all with bathing, boating and fishing. Golf course on headland. The small village of Porth Dinllaen (along beach or walk over golf course) is well worth a visit, has a pub and a lifeboat station.

---

under any obvious protection, it is well worth making the effort to see, but on account of lack of care by visitors, it has over the last few years shown a visible deterioration.

From the site the highest peak is easily reached by an easy path which leads from the south end of Tre'r Ceiri down to a shallow valley and up to the highest peak on the Lleyn. The views

are extensive — note down at the foot of the mountain perched almost on the edge of the sea a small village in a dark valley. This is Nant Gwrtheyrn, a tiny hamlet once dependent on quarrying, which can be reached only by foot down a steep and winding road, There is a convenient car park at the end of the road leading seawards from the crossroads in Llithfaen. The des-

Places of Interest Near Nefyn

Tre'r-Ceiri
Britain's oldest city with walls. Built on the crown of a hill. Remains of 250 or so stone huts surrounded by several walls. Built about 3,000-4,000 years ago. Worth the effort of seeing. By the footpath, leave the B4417 at top of the hill between Llithfaen and Llanaelhaearn north of Nefyn.

Nant Gwrtheyrn
In ancient Vortigerns Valley, accessible old quarrying village on sea side of Rivals. An idyllic spot with small beach. Being renovated as a centre for Welsh studies. Approach only on foot, about 3/4 mile from car park. Turn off in centre of village of Llithfaen towards the sea, off B4417, 5 miles north of Nefyn.

L
2h
*
ooo

cent from the car park on foot for about 1 mile brings one to a village of utter peace and quiet without motor cars. The village is simply two lines of cottages set around a square and the inevitable chapel. After lying in ruins for many years the cottages are now being renovated to provide a centre for Welsh language studies. Below is a fine stretch of sandy beach.

The climb back to the car park is a reminder of the plight of the earlier inhabitants and their weekly visit to the shops. The valley is steep-sided and sometimes sombre, the reason perhaps for its other name, Vortigern's Valley. Legend has it that Vortigern, one time British King, took refuge here before being struck down by heavenly fire.

The northern side of the hills are less interesting on account of extensive quarrying around Trevor. On the road to Caernarfon the church of Clynnog Fawr is worthy of interest. Founded by St Beuno in AD616, it is one of the mother churches of Wales. Until the Dissolution it was a monastery, but the present church dates only from the sixteenth century. It con-

Places of Interest on the Northern Coast of Lleyn

Clynnog Fawr Church
One of the first churches in Wales, dedicated to St Beuno. The rebuilt church stands on the site of an ancient monastery. Contains many old relics. On A499 south of Caernarfon. Close to the church in an old burial site interesting because the capstone is carved with hundreds of cups.

Dinas Dinlle
Oval mound with ramparts and ditch, an ancient defensive spot used by both British and Romans. Off A499, towards Llandwrog about 5 miles south of Caernarfon.

Fort Belan
Eighteenth-century fort with cannons, maritime museum and old forge. Tea rooms and gift shop with pottery. Train rides, horse rides and even plane rides above the mountains of Snowdonia. Something for everyone. As above but continue past mound to aerodrome and headland.

Museum of Old Welsh County Life
Tai'n Lon, Clynnafgawr, 10 miles south of Caernarfon. Housed in seventeenth-century corn mill.

tains many relics of the early saint and he is traditionally buried there. Nearby is a much older burial site. Close to the shore and just west of the church is an ancient burial chamber with a capstone about 6ft high by 8ft long and 5ft wide carved with hundreds of cups.

The coast continues northwards towards the Menai Straits with an ancient site, and a much more recent one to visit. Taking the road to Llandwrog and to the tip of the Straits you pass the conspicuous Iron Age fort of Dinas Dinlle. It is roughly oval with two ramparts and a ditch, and was probably also used by the Romans. Further on, at the very tip of the headland, is the eighteenth-century Fort Belan, built by Thomas Wynne (Lord Newborough) and garrisoned by a force of 400 men which he raised and equipped at his own expense. It was intended to defend Caernarfon from the French, during the Napoleonic wars and as such it was a magnanimous gesture that nearly broke him. Today the Fort is one of the area's newest attractions. Besides the building and many of the original features, it has a mini-railway, a pottery, a café and a gift shop. There is something for the whole family — even a light aeroplane for trips over the area and mountains.

Caernarfon is the starting and finishing point for many journeys. To the south the peninsula stretches its arm lazily towards Ireland, its coastline one of the finest in Europe.

Porth Neigwl (Hells Mouth) with its four mile beach and bay

7 Anglesey -
The Isle of Mona

Anglesey is the largest island off the coast of Wales and England. Although separated only by the Menai Straits, which vary from several hundred yards to several miles in width, it retains all the character of an island. The climate is generally milder and drier than that of the mainland nearby, making it ideal for seaside holidays. There are many sandy beaches easily accessible for swimming or boating.

Many visitors to the island will be aware of its prehistoric connections with the Druids and Celtic Christianity, for legend and fact about the past are inextricably mixed. Perhaps like modern visitors the early settlers found the climate more amenable than the mainland and the nearby mountains. There is much evidence of early man's use of the land, and visitors are today welcomed to the island by the sign *'Mon, Mam Cymru* — Anglesey, Mother of Wales'. This title comes from the island's early fertility and farming habits. It was always a major supplier of grain to the rest of Wales, for it was said that more grain was

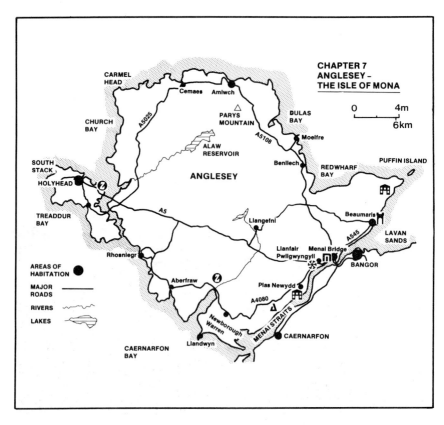

*Menai Straits with Telford's Bridge and
Church Island*

Brittania Bridge

BR 4405/4

BRITISH RAILWAYS BOARD (M)

LLANFAIRPWLLGWYNGYLLGOGERYCHWYRNDROBWLLLLANTYSILIOGOGOGOCH

SOUVENIR PLATFORM TICKET 10p.

AVAILABLE ONE HOUR ON DAY OF ISSUE ONLY
NOT VALID IN TRAINS NOT TRANSFERABLE

FOR CONDITIONS SEE OVER

L 59847
L 59847

| 1 | 2 | 3 | 4 | 5 | 6 | 7 | 8 | 9 | 10 | 11 | 12 |

The longest platform ticket in the world

grown in Anglesey, the smallest county, than in the rest of the country. Today many of the fields are only pasture land.

Compared with the nearby mountains of Snowdonia, the island is flat, the highest point being just over 500ft above sea level. Geographically there are some fine examples of ancient rocks including Pre-Cambrian, sandstone and limestone that come to the surface at several places. The main attraction, however, is its coastline, with its sandy beaches and quiet coves.

The Menai straits, though narrow, are notorious for the tides that race through them and have made the crossing until recently fraught with difficulty. There were at one time seven ferries across the Straits all greatly overcharging for the short trip. The most common route was on foot across the Lavan Sands near Bangor and then by ferry across the remaining water to Beaumaris. Cattle going to market were forced to swim across, urged on by the drovers in the boats, but losses were high and life dangerous.

Today's visitor is more fortunate,

for in 1826 Thomas Telford completed his remarkable suspension bridge as part of the London to Holyhead road. Faced with the problem of bridging the Straits but allowing room for the tall fully rigged sailing ships to pass underneath, he built the world's second chain suspension bridge. The towers of locally quarried limestone held the massive chains which were anchored into the solid rock at each end, with the road suspended below on wrought iron rods. For the first time it became possible to cross to and from the mainland with dry feet for a small toll charge, and stage coaches and mail coaches made the bridge an instant success. The graceful lines of the bridge were unfortunately not designed for twentieth-century loads and in 1936 major strengthening took place. Though not detracting from the appearance of the bridge, it has enabled it to cope with today's traffic.

The neighbouring Britannia Bridge had an equally illustrious past. Another great engineer, Robert Stephenson, built the railway between London and Holyhead for the Irish Ferry. Faced also with the problem of sailing ships he solved it by constructing two parallel cast-iron tubes high above the water between three towers, at the time a unique solution. Opened in 1850 and in continuous use until 1970, when it was accidentally destroyed by fire, it was a tribute to the foresight of the Victorian engineers. The remodelled Britannia Bridge has a level for trains and an upper level for road traffic and though perhaps not as graceful as the earlier bridge it has at least lightened the load of Telford's Suspension Bridge and eased the traffic-flow problem in summer. Much of Stephenson's original work remains incorporated in the new bridge.

The first Marquess of Anglesey greets all visitors to the island as they cross the straits. From high on his column of local limestone he surveys his domain and casts an approving eye over the two bridges. Inside there are steps up to a balustrade surrounding the top. It provides a dizzy vantage point from which to survey the island, the Straits and the mountains of Snowdonia , but it is not for the acrophobic. Unfortunately the Marquess never saw the statue, for he died at the age of 86, five years before it was completed. He rose to fame as the Duke of Wellington's second in command at the Battle of Waterloo. As Lord Paget, he had been accompanying the duke from the battlefield when a cannon ball smashed his leg. 'By God, sir, I've lost my leg' he shouted to the Duke. 'By God, sir, so you have'

Places of Interest Around Menai

Llanfairpwllgwyngyllgogerychwyrndrobwllllantysiliogogogoch
Village with the world's longest place name, also the longest platform ticket in the world, available at the railway station souvenir shop.

Marquess of Anglesey's Column
90ft-tall with statue on top comemorating the First Marquess, Lord Paget. Views from platform of mountains and Menai Straits are superb.

Plas Newydd
Home of Marquess of Anglesey, on edge of Straits, with many fine pictures and also mementoes of the Battle of Waterloo. Beautiful grounds. Off A4080 two miles from Llanfair PG.

Toll house, Llanfair PG
Last to operate, until 1895, still displays tolls. On A5 at start of village.

Plas Goch Leisure Park
Caravan site, swimming pool, picnic areas and mini golf. Many other attractions including restaurant and disco in evening. On side of Straits next door to Plas Newyd.

Bryn-Celli-Ddu
Best preserved burial mound with huge stones and passage. Probably early Bronze Age. 1½ mile north of A4080 to Llanddaniel Fab, walk up farm track.

Brynsiencyn
There are many ancient sites in the fields around the village including burial chambers and earthworks.

Brynsiencyn Pottery
In centre of the village off A4080

replied Wellington, and resumed surveying the retreating French. For his bravery at that battle he was created the First Marquess of Anglesey. With his family he lived at Plas Newydd just a mile away and despite his wooden leg he continued to have a successful career in government.

The A5, which we have used already in North Wales, crosses the two bridges and runs by the Marquess's feet. It then turns inland to cross the island, and very soon arrives at probably the most famous village in Anglesey. Known throughout Britain for having the longest name is Llanfairpwllgwyn quite simply Llanfair PG. The name was further extended to a total of 58 letters by a local wit at the end of the last century, presumably for the benefit of tourists. The tiny station has the doubtful distinction of issuing the longest platform ticket in the world and probably also having the longest sign.

By the side of the road on the way into the village is an octagonal tollhouse designed by Telford. It was the last tollhouse to operate in the country, finally opening its gates in 1895, and it still bears the sign stating the tolls. This attractive building is a tribute to the genius of the engineer who did everything so well.

The A5 continues its journey to its destination at Holyhead almost bisect-

Telford's Octagonal
Tollhouse in
Llanfairpwllgwyngyll
still displaying tolls

ing the island in the process. It is not a particularly exciting drive, for the scenery is fairly plain and the road seems to stretch endlessly in front. Unless one is dashing to the ferry to Ireland or off to climb the sea cliffs on Holy Island it is infinitely more pleasant to take the less auspicious roads that follow the coast.

It is convenient to start from the Anglesey column and take the A4080 which runs parallel with the Menai Straits. After about a mile is the house of Plas Newydd between the road and the Straits. One may take the opportunity to relax in the tranquil gardens and take in the magnificent views across the mountains. Plas Newydd was the home of the First Marquess of Anglesey, and it now has a small museum devoted to his military career with some mementoes of Waterloo. It was built in the eighteenth century by James Wyatt, and there are some fine rooms, furniture and portraits, in-

cluding some important works by Rex Whistler. Outside, the lawns slope down to the sea wall. During the summer a boat service from the quay at Caernarfon offers trips along the straits to the house, a most unusual approach.

Nearby is the Plas Goch Leisure Park, which seems to have something for everybody — a heated outdoor swimming pool, play and picnic areas, bars, cafés and a caravan park. All this is situated in the 200 acres of parkland surrounding the fifteenth-century Manor House. With a direct frontage on to the Straits it is also well equipped for watersports.

On the opposite side of the road to Plas Goch, and up a short lane, is the chambered cairn of Bryn-Celli-Ddu. This is the best preserved of all the burial chambers on Anglesey and is easily accessible on foot from the road. Originally 160ft in diameter and covering the whole of the area inside

Bryn-Celli-Ddu burial mound

the fenced enclosure, little was found when it was excavated in 1928. The stone chamber dates from about 2000 BC but the covering mound is a modern weather protection. From the car park is a gateway to the farm and it is a short walk along the lane to the cairn.

This southern corner of the island has many similar burial chambers, though none quite as well preserved as Bryn-Celli-Ddu. It does indicate that this was probably the most inhabited part of the island in ancient times. The sea is nearby, the land is flat and it was not as tree-covered as elsewhere. Stories of Druids are well known and give Anglesey a reputation it has never quite lived down. They were not the fearsome people we have come to expect, but the religious leaders of a particular sect, living on the island to escape persecution by the Romans. The burial chambers and cairns in the area probably even pre-date the Druids and are not, as many people imagine, the sacrificial altars of these notorious priests. Though there is in fact very little evidence of their reli-

gious monuments, it is known that this particular corner of the island was their headquarters in the early centuries AD.

No love was lost between the Romans and Druids, and after a fearsome battle on the very edge of the Straits the Romans succeeded in invading the island. They destroyed everything connected with the religion and subdued the people. It was not until several centuries after the withdrawal of the Romans that Anglesey re-established itself as a religious centre with the coming of Christianity.

Newborough, or more particularly the area beyond the village to the sea, is not one of the busiest parts of the island but it is certainly one of the nicest. From the centre of the village a narrow road goes out, the forest behind the town. There is a charge to enter the forest by road, which gives access to one of the finest beaches in North Wales, with car parks and picnic spots.

The forest is one vast nature reserve covering the sand dunes and salt

Visitor Centre on Llandwyn Island looking across Caernarfon Bay to the Rivals

---

Places of Interest on Southern Side of Anglesey

Newborough Warren
Superb beach surrounded by forest with many forest trails and picnic spots. Access to car park behind dunes (small toll).

Llanddwyn
Approach across beach from Newborough Warren. A peninsular of Pre-Cambrian rock, now a nature reserve, with old cottages, lifeboat station and lighthouse. A grand spot for views of the hills across the bay. Off A4080 in Newborough Village.

Aberffraw
Sandy beach with island church of St Cwfan on site of early Celtic church.

Glantraeth Zoo Garden
Collection of small animals in private grounds. Ideal for children, also farm museum and restaurant. Off B4422 between Newborough and Aberffraw

Rhosneigr
Sandy beaches ideal for bathing and boating. Popular resort with many areas for birdwatching around the village.

Valley
Car park near RAF aerodrome for 'plane spotters'. Jet trainers and helicopters can be seen coming and going frequently. Off A5 before crossing to Holy Island.

---

marshes behind the sea shore. Known as Newborough Warren for the number of rabbits which used to live there — 80,000 were trapped annually — the dunes cover the old village of Rhosyr and its field system. It is hoped that the trees and grasses recently planted will stabilise the drifting sands. There are several paths and nature trails through the reserve and visitors should stay on the marked paths. A leaflet of information is available on the site.

Besides the extensive forests there is a huge beach and foreshore with fine golden sands. It is close to the car park and is never crowded, stretching for several miles in each direction. It is a short walk across the beach to Llanddwyn Island, a promontory connected to the mainland by a narrow strip of rock. The island is a nature reserve criss-crossed by easily followed foot paths. Many wild flowers grow in the grass and undergrowth: visitors are asked to stay on the paths. Birds can be seen resting around the island's cliffs, and there are superb views of the mainland hills.

On the tip of the island is a lighthouse and lifeboat station above a small bay. The lifeboatmen's cottages have been renovated as a visitor centre where there are leaflets giving an outline of the flora and fauna in the area. The adjacent cottages are furnished in original style giving a glimpse of eighteenth-century life there. There are several more miles of beach with Malltraeth sands to the north of the island, all accessible from the car park. The area is highly recommended for a fascinating day out.

Until the building of an embankment connecting Newborough with Malltraeth the estuary of the Afon Cefni almost cut the island in half. Now the low lying land is being turned into pastureland, with the estuary on the seaward side of the embankment silting up to create even more expanses of sand at low tide, teeming with wildfowl and waders.

Aberffraw, just beyond Newborough, was for many centuries the capital of Gwynedd and home of the Welsh Princes. Nothing remains today of their palaces, though a Norman arch in the church of St Beuno is traditionally said to have been built by them. The village, a busy port before the coming of the railways, is now a popular holiday centre with some fine beaches and rocky headlands. Accessible at low tide is the tiny church of St Cwyfan, built on a small island. It is thought to have been founded originally in the seventh century but was extensively rebuilt in 1893.

The bays to the north were the haunt of the eighteenth-century wreckers who lured ships on to the nearby rocks. Today they are the haunt of yachtsmen and weekend sailors, as some of them are particularly suitable for canoe surfing. Rhosneigr stands between two beautiful bays, both excellent for swimming and water sports. It was a popular Edwardian resort, and has remained so to this day as an ideal family holiday town. The extensive area of gorse: covered dunes just to the north is Tywyn Trewan Common, a paradise for birdwatchers and botanists.

For those who prefer to watch the creations of modern technology the nearby RAF aerodrome at Valley is the home of the RAF advanced jet flying school and the regional centre for the air/sea rescue service. Aircraft and helicopters are coming and going all day long, many on training flights, and there is a car park for plane spotters. The airfield was originally built in 1941 as a terminal for trans-Atlantic crossings for the USAF. During the construction a large cache of bronze

Roman Walls of Caer Gybi in Holyhead

weapons and other implements were found in a lake. Known as the Llyn Cerrig Bach hoard, it is now in the National Museum of Wales and is thought to have been votive offerings for Iron Age religious ceremonies.

Across the bay is Holy Island, separated by a narrow strip of water from the main island, and for many centuries the religious centre of Anglesey. Thought to have been the religious stronghold of the Druids, it was settled in the sixth century by St Cybi who built a small church within the remains of the Roman Fort at Holyhead. He was a formidable character who travelled the whole of Anglesey converting the people. There is still a church dedicated to him within the walls of the Roman Fort at Holyhead, but it is a much more recent building with some fine carved stonework. The town of Holyhead is still known in Welsh as Caergybi, Gybi's fortress.

Holyhead is a bustling town, which has grown to be the largest in Anglesey. It is basically a seaport servicing the busy Irish Ferry boats and the recently developing trade in container ships. The town surrounds the harbour and is gradually spreading up the slopes of Holyhead mountain. Holyhead is also developing as a yachting centre with a pleasant shingle beach and safe mooring, protected by a long breakwater. A promenade, running along its full length, makes it also extremely popular for sea fisherman.

It has been difficult to avoid the busy A5 trunk road as it carves its way so impressively through the heart of North Wales, particularly as several of the bridges are so significant in the development of the area and are impressive features in their own right. At last in Holyhead the road finally reaches its destination and terminates at triumphal arch on the quayside, just 267 miles from Marble Arch in London — a triumph of engineering.

Behind the town, Holyhead Mountain rises gently to the low banks of an ancient hill fort of indeterminate age on its summit. Much of the headland is a nature reserve controlled by the Royal Society for the Protection of Birds. The steep cliffs and hillsides are a favourite nesting place for many seabirds including puffins, guillemots, gulls and razorbills. During June and July the rare auk may also be seen there. Perhaps the best place to observe the birds is from the area around South Stack Lighthouse.

In a magnificent setting the lighthouse has a true 'Land's End' feel about it. Surrounded by steep cliffs, it can be approached down 379 steps from a car park. They are the best way to see the superb cliff faces around the lighthouse and observe the birds. The rocks offer some of the hardest climbing in Wales for many climbers from the mainland; except in the nesting season they vie with the seabirds for every little ledge and handhold. The lighthouse is on a small island at the bottom of the cliffs, approached across a small suspension bridge. it is open to the public each afternoon during the summer. For the statistically minded the lighthouse is automatic, 91ft high and 197ft above high water. Built in 1808 by David Alexander, who also built Dartmoor Prison, it is probably the most visited lighthouse in Britain.

L
1h
*
oooo

Just below the car park and perched on the very edge of the cliffs is a squat square building that has been for many years an ugly ruin. Known as Ellen's Tower it was built in 1868 by the Rt Hon Owen Stanley (MP for Penrhos) as a place to enjoy the view. Recently it has been converted by the Royal Society for the Protection of Birds into an observatory for birdwatchers for there are fine views of the

South Stack lighthouse and the cliffs

cliffs. It provides a welcome refuge from the wind for ornithologists and other visitors.

The whole of the South Stack area is full of interest. Alongside the approach road to the lighthouse is a fine collection of hut circles. They are the remains of twenty huts of various shapes and sizes believed to be part of a much larger settlement. Easily accessible from the road they give a good idea of how our ancestors lived, showing signs of their sleeping slabs and hearths. Now in the care of the state, they perpetuate in the name Cythiau'r Gwyddelod, or Irishmen's Walls, the belief that they were built by settlers from across the sea, although there is no evidence to substantiate this. Nearby are two large standing stones, which are thought to have been the centre stones of a much larger circle, although they now stand alone. Throughout Holy Island there are many other standing stones and hut circles, perhaps indicating that it

was after all the centre of religion long before Christianity arrived.

To the south of Holyhead there are several popular holiday resorts, particularly Trearddur Bay which sits astride the pre-Telford road to the island. It has several fine beaches with golden sands and rocky outcrops just offshore, making it popular with skin divers and water skiers, though it can be windy. Rhoscolyn, on the southern tip, equally popular for water sports, is more sheltered from the wind. From the village there are some fine cliff; top walks particularly to the well of St Gwenfaen which is reputed to be able to cure mental illness. The nearby cliffs have rock formations showing the bending and folding which took place during the earth's formation.

Back on Anglesey the coast to the north with its small bays and rocky coves is very reminiscent of Cornwall. All the beaches give good views across the bay to Holy Island and Holyhead. Church Bay is perhaps the most

Things to do on Holy Island

Beaches
Holyhead: Sand and shingle beach inside harbour breakwater (1½ mile long).
Trearddur Bay: Fine sands with rocky outcrops, ideal for bathing and many water sports
Rhoscolyn: Sandy beaches with good sheltered bathing. Fine cliff walks.
Silver Bay: Sandy beach near mouth of channel between the two islands.

Holyhead
Roman walls surrounding church of St Gybi, near town centre. Triumphal arch to celebrate completion of A5 and visit of George IV. Busy port for Irish Ferries protected by 1½-mile breakwater with road along. Ideal for fishing.

South Stack Lighthouse
Steps down give magnificent views of cliffs with nesting birds and rock climbers. Lighthouse open in afternoons during summer.

Ellen's Tower
Bird observatory overlooking South Stack Lighthouse and cliffs, just below the car park for the lighthouse. All the headland is owned by the RSPB. Care should be taken when walking in the area.

Holyhead Mountain Hut Circles
Remains of an extensive settlement of second-fourth centuries. Circular and square huts, once thatched. Some have central hearths and upright slabs showing positions of beds and seats. By road to South Stack.

Penrhos-Feilw Standing Stones
Two stones believed to be the remains of a larger circle. 1¾ mile south west of Holyhead. There are several other standing stones on the island for those interested in these antiquities.

Penrhos
Nature reserve with woodlands and sea birds. Nature trails. Off A5 south of Holyhead.

visited beach on that stretch of coast. This north-west corner of the island is dominated by the hill of Mynydd Y Garn, which, like any hill surrounded by flat land, appears much higher than it is. A road runs very close to the top leaving but a short walk to the gorse-topped summit. The views are of the nearby coast, Carmel Head and the Wylfa Power Station. Off Carmel Head can be seen The Skerries, a small group of islets used by breeding birds and seals. The lighthouse on The Skerries has been there since the eight-eenth century and was one of the early examples that extracted a toll from every passing ship.

East of the headland the cliffs seem to get wilder until Cemlyn Bay is reached. The sheltered beach, owned by the National Trust, once the haunt of pirates, is now a bird sanctuary. Visitors are requested to take care during the nesting season (April-June), if they use the cliff top walks around the bay and headland. Much of this northern coast, however, is dominated by the massive bulk of the

Amlwch Harbour

Wylfa Nuclear Power Station. As the power station is in an area of outstanding natural beauty, the Central Electricity Generating Board has provided a nature trail around the headland. There is also an observation tower for looking over the power station and surroundings, while during the summer visitors can tour the site (by appointment).

Several little harbours along the northern coast are worth visiting. The nearest to Wylfa is Cemaes Bay; its tiny harbour and pleasant beach are well sheltered from all but the northern-most winds. The cliffs alongside the bay are National Trust property with some pleasant walks, particularly along to Llanbadrig. The church above the cliffs is dedicated to St Patrick and is believed to be on the site of one of the oldest churches in Anglesey. It is said that Patrick was shipwrecked on the little island of Middle Mouse just a short distance from the headland. He established a church here as thanksgiving for his salvation before leaving to convert the people of Ireland.

Amlwch, a little further east, has a fine little harbour, built of unmortared rock placed vertically rather than horizontally. It is small and narrow, owing its fame to the nearby Parys Mountain copper mine. During the heyday of the mine, it became the main port for the export of copper and the remains of the old quays can still be seen. Ships were built at the port after the decline of the copper industry and the remains of the old slipways can be seen. It has now become a major oil port. At the Anglesey Marine Terminal 2 miles offshore, crude oil tankers of more than 500,000 tons can moor and discharge their cargo. It is pumped directly ashore and through an underground pipeline to Stanlow, 78 miles away in Cheshire, where it is

---

Beaches and Places of Interest Along the North Coast of Anglesey

Church Bay
Partly sand with rocky outcrops, good views across to Holy Island and Holyhead. Fine cliff walks.

Carmel Head
Rocky coves with good cliff walks

Cemlyn Bay
Steep shelving pebble beach

Cemaes Bay
Fine harbour and sandy bay. Good swimming and cliff walks to Llanbadrig and church. Overlooked by Wylfa Nuclear Power Station, open to visitors in summer.

Bull Bay
Rocky cove with sheltered bathing and good walks

Amlwch
Small narrow harbour, old port for nearby copper mines of Parys Mountain. Swimming pool in town.

Parys Mountain
Eighteenth-century copper mines, now a mountain of waste. Some interesting coloured rocks to be seen, but care must be taken.

Llyn Alaw
Visitor centre and fishing on reservoir. Off B5112 at Llanerchymedd.

---

refined. The harbour has had a new lease of life servicing the terminal and has been expanded.

Inland from Amlwch are the scarred remains of Parys Mountain. Once the biggest open cast copper mine in the world, it produced 80,000 tons of ore per year until the early nineteenth century. In the eighteenth century the output was so great as almost to cause the collapse of the whole of Cornwall's great copper mining industry. Visitors must beware of the dangerous shafts and waste heaps around the scattered workings. Efforts are being made to work the mine again, though now it is a blot on the surrounding countryside.

Further inland, behind the mountain, is Llyn Alaw, a fairly new reservoir much favoured by trout fishermen. The church at nearby Llanbabo has three grotesque carved faces above the door, while inside is a finely carved slab believed to date from the fourteenth century. There are also several standing stones and burial mounds around the lake. One in particular, known as Bedd Branwen (Branwen's grave), is traditionally the burying place of Branwen mentioned in the Welsh folk legends *The Mabinogion*.

The eastern side of the island is extremely popular for family holidays. Most of the beaches are well sheltered, with good stretches of fine golden sands and safe bathing. Behind, the countryside is more rolling than elsewhere, with trees more noticeable than on the windy north and west coasts.

Traeth Dulas to the north is a quiet estuary and land-locked bay. Quite out of place are the remains of the old brickworks established in the heyday of Parys Mountain, presumably to cash in on the lucrative building projects. The nearby beaches of Traeth Lligwy are excellent, backed by sand dunes.

On the approach roads to the beaches overlooking the bay are several antiquities well worth visiting. They are all signposted from the main

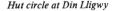
Hut circle at Din Lligwy

Beaches and Places of Interest on the Eastern Coast of Anglesey

Traeth Dulas
Land-locked bay with sandy beach. Also remains of old brickworks from heyday of nearby Parys Mountain.

Traeth Lligwy
Sandy beach backed by dunes and fields. Nearby is Iron Age village of Din Lligwy, a short walk across fields to walled village with remains of hut circles, a pleasant stroll. Also Capel Lligwy, a church standing above headland. Nearby is a Neolithic (Stone Age) burial chamber with massive capstone. All are just by the road ½ mile north of Llanallgo church.

Moelfre
Boat hire, sailing and water skiiing. Pebble beach.

Benllech
Long sandy beach, with donkey rides, deckchairs and cafés. Very popular

Red Wharf Bay
Wide bay with long walk to the sea when the tide is out. Good sand and good bathing at high tide.

road and all can be seen at any time with only a short easy walk. The largest is Din Lligwy, probably the fourth-century fortified residence of a native chieftain. Now surrounded by woods it is a fine example, with much of the floor plan and walls evident. On the same walk is Capel Lligwy, a church of obscure origin but in a superb situa-tion. Just a short distance along the road is the Lligwy Burial Chamber, with an impressive capstone of solid limestone about 15ft square and 3ft thick, supported on a ring of upright rock 'posts'. It is thought to have been in use in the Early Bronze Age, about 2,000BC.

Moelfre, out on the headland, has boats for hire, and, a pebbly beach which is good for water skiing and sailing. The lifeboat station has been involved in many famous disasters; perhaps the best known is the *Royal Charter* which went down nearby with the loss of 452 lives in 1859. To the south, the beaches of Benllech and Red Wharf Bay are probably the most popular on the island. They are long and sandy, and at low tide Red Wharf Bay is an extensive estuary. Benllech has donkey rides, deck chairs and sea-front cafés. There are several caravan sites along this section of coast.

Stretching out towards the mainland is Penmon head, with Puffin Island just offshore. The coast is scarred by the remains of old limestone quarries, but the headland is a pretty spot. It can be approached through Penmon Priory whose remains, mainly eleventh century, are adjacent to the road and there is a fine dovecote. Much of the priory is still in use, the abbot's house is still inhabited and the attached church still a parish church. Just behind the buildings is the well of St Seiriol, an early Celtic saint active on the island at the same time as St Cybi. Around the well are a few small buildings and the remains of an oval hut, possibly the early saint's cell.

For a small toll you can drive to the coastguard station and café at Trwyn Du or Black Point just opposite Puffin Island. It is a grand spot and with the mournful toll of the bell on the lighthouse one can easy conjure up

Penmon Priory and Dovecoat

thoughts of shipwrecks. The island, also known as Priestholme or Ynys Seiriol, once had a small monastery, later moved to Penmon Priory — and of course many puffins. The bird population declined on account of the popularity of pickled young birds in the early nineteenth century. At the point, there are some small sandy beaches and excellent views across to the mountains of Snowdonia, particularly the Carneddau. On the south is the entrance to the Menai Straits and across the bay are the Lavan Sands, once the main route to the island.

It was to command this route into Anglesey that Edward I built a castle at Beaumaris, almost on the edge of the Straits. It is small compared with its two near neighbours at Conwy and Caernarfon, but around it are the remains of a moat which once connected the castle to the sea. Because of its lowlying situation it does not at first sight seem impressive but it is in fact one of the most complete and best designed castles built during Edward's reign. Despite its solid defences it has seen little trouble, a short occupation by the Welsh during Owain Glyndwr's uprising in 1404 probably being the high point of its career. Nevertheless it is a charming little castle, with a children's playground against the outside wall.

Opposite the entrance to the castle is the courthouse built in 1614. Still in its original state and still in use, it is furnished as it was built with the coat of arms of James I over the bench and the public area separated by massive iron bars. Until the last century it was the main Assize Court for the county but since 1971 it has been only a magistrates' court. It is the oldest courhouse in the country and it is said that the notorious Judge Jefferies once held an Assize here. An equally fascinating place for those unfamiliar with the ways of justice is Beaumaris Jail. Built in 1829, it still has all the cells, the punishment cell and a treadwheel unique in Britain. There is much of interest and one is reminded of the harshness of our early penal system.

The town has several other interesting buildings in its narrow streets, including the Bull's Head Hotel, a favourite with visiting judges and believed to have played host to General Mytton, Cromwell's general during his Anglesey campaign, Dr Johnson and Charles Dickens. The church of St Mary and St Nicholas is almost as old as the castle and has many interesting features. Above the town is the obelisk memorial to the Bulkeley family, once the biggest landowners on the island, whose home at Baron Hill is now an overgrown ruin.

Beaumaris plays host each August to the Straits Regatta, a major yachting event organised by the Royal Anglesey Yacht Club. The town has something for everyone: bowls, tennis, fishing and many elegant buildings.

By comparison, Menai Bridge seems a busy little town crouching below Telford's suspension bridge. To suit children of all ages, including grownups, is the Museum of Childhood near the town centre, with some fine displays of toys, games and furniture. The Tegfryn Art Gallery has regular shows by Welsh artists. Along the Belgian Promenade, built by refugees during World War I, there are several pleasant walks to Church Island, out in the Straits, which is easily reached by a causeway.

With the building of the two bridges, much of the importance of the towns along the Straits was re-

Puffin Island

Beaumaris Castle and moat

moved. Holyhead became the biggest and most important town and Llangefni, almost in the centre of the island, took over the role of administrative centre from Beaumauris. Llangefni is a bustling market town with wide streets (market day Thursday), situated on the Afon Cefni by which it could once be reached by boat. There are some pleasant walks in the vicinity of the town. However, most visitors to the island come to see the coastline and the beaches, and will probably spend little time in the interior. There is something for everybody on Anglesey and there is always the probability of warmer weather than on the mainland.

Places of Interest Along Menai Straits

Penmon Priory and Dovecote
Medieval monastery still partly in use as house and church. Dovecote is sixteenth century with room for 1,000 nests. Good solid stone building with domed roof. On road from Beaumaris to Puffin Island.

St Seriol's Well, Penmon
Holy Well close to Priory with some stone walls possibly of the orignal saint's cell. About sixth century. Short walk from Priory.

Puffin Island
Just off Black Point, lighthouse with melancholy bell, coastguard station with café and pebbly beach. A lonely spot. Along road past Penmon Priory (small toll).

Church of St Tysilio
On island in Menai Straits accessible by causeway from Belgian walks.

Tegfryn Art Gallery, Cadnant Road, Menai Bridge
Exhibitions by Welsh artists.

Belgian Walks, Menai Bridge
Constructed by Belgian refugees during World War I as a promenade. Gives good views of Telford's Suspension Bridge.

Museum of Childhood, Menai Bridge
Fascinating collection of toys, games and other things that have held children's interest throughout the ages. Suitable for all ages and situated in Water Street.

Beaumaris Castle
Last of Edward I's mighty forts, once accessible by sea, now well preserved and not aggressive looking. Children's playground next to it.

Beaumaris Courthouse
Oldest courthouse in the country still in use. All the original furniture and fittings still intact, very interesting if you are unfamiliar with such buildings. Opposite castle.

Beaumaris Jail
Built in 1829 and still as it was, with treadwheel and cells. All the work rooms and exercise yards and punishment blocks are complete.

The Language

The visitor to Wales will see place names that are different and will hear people speak in a very different language. This can be baffling to the non-Welsh speaker, while finding your way around can be a daunting task particularly if you have to ask your way.

Many place names are descriptive of the physical feature of the area, eg, Moelwyn Mawr, the big bare hill.

Others are named after the local church; hence the predominance of the names preceded by Llan, church of, as in Llanbadrig, Church of Patrick. It can add interest and enjoyment to any holiday to try to solve the mystery of the language and find out where you are. A few words that may be useful are given below; most are found in place names.

Aber	- river mouth	Clwyd	- gate
Adwy	- gap, pass	Coed	- trees
Afon	- river	Craig	- rock
Allt	- wooded hill or cliff	Crib	- ridge
Aran	- high place, mountain	Croes	- cross, cross-roads
		Din, Dinas	- fort
Bach	- small, corner	Dre	- homestead
Bala	- joining of lake to river	Drws	- door, pass
		Du, Ddu	- black
Banc	- bank, hill	Dwy	- two
Bedd	- grave	Dyffryn	- valley
Bont	- bridge		
Bron	- breast of hill or slope	Eglwys	- church
		Erw	- acre
Bryn	- hill	Esgair	- long ridge
Bwlch	- pass or col		
Bychan	- small	Fach	- small
		Fawr	- large, great, extensive
Cader	- seat, stronghold	Fechan	- small
Cae	- field	Ffair	- fair
Caer	- fort	Fford	- road
Capel	- chapel	Ffraw	- rapid
Carn	- cairn	Ffrith	- meadow
Carreg	- stone	Foel	- bare hill
Carrog	- stream	Fychan	- small
Cefn	- ridge		
Celli	- grove	Garth	- hill
Clogwyn	- cliff, precipice	Glan	- brink, edge
		Glas	- blue, green

Glyder	- sheltered valley	Nos	- night
Glyn	- valley	Ogof	- cave
Gwydd	- trees		
Gwyddfa	- wild place	Penrhyn	- headland
Gwynt	- wind	Pant	- hollow ground
		Parc	- field
Hafod	- summer home	Penmaen	- rocky headland
Hen	- old	Pennant	- head of valley
Hendre	- winter home	Pentre	- village, hamlet
Hyll	- ugly	Pig	- summit
		Pistyll	- cataract
Isaf	- lower	Plas	- hall
		Pont	- bridge
Llain	- stretch of land	Porth	- harbour, bay
Llan	- church or enclosed space		
Llanerch	- clearing glade	Rhos	- moorland
Llech	- stone slab	Rhyd	- ford
Llety	- small house		
Llyn	- lake	Saeth	- arrow
		Sarn	- causeway
Maen	- stone		
Maes	- field	Tal	- front
Mam	- mother	Tan	- below
Mawr	- great, extensive	Traeth	- beach
Melin	- mill	Tyn	- small farm
Merch (plural Merchedd)	- woman	Tywyn	- shore
Moel	- bare or rounded mountain	Uchaf	- upper
Morfa	- coastal marsh	Wen	- white
Mynydd	- mountain	Y	- the
		Yr	- the
Nant	- brook, valley	Ynys	- island
Neuadd	- hall	Ysbyty	- hospital
Newydd	- new	Ystryd	- street

Further Information for Visitors

Castles are generally so dominant in a town that no addresses have been given. Most are open throughout the year and to some of the smaller ones there is no charge for admission (marked F).

Towns with castles:-

Beaumaris
Caernarfon
Conwy
Criccieth
Denbigh
Dolwyddelan (F)
Ewloe (F)
Flint
Harlech
Hawarden
Llanberis (F)
Llangollen (F)
Rhuddlan

HOUSES AND GARDENS OPEN TO THE PUBLIC

Generally open daily between April and September.

Erddig House, (National Trust), Wrexham
Off A438, 1 mile south of Wrexham. Open April-October, 12pm-5.30pm, closed Monday.
Agricultural museum, restaurant.

Plas Newydd, Llangollen
1 mile south of town centre. Open May-September

Bodrhydan Hall, Rhuddlan
3 miles south east of Rhyl. Open June-September Tuesday and Thursday afternoons.

Gwyrch Castle, Abergele
1 mile south east of town centre. Tel: Abergele 825007
Open each afternoon mid May-mid September. Café, walks and amusements.

Aberconwy House (National Trust), Conwy.
Junction of High Street and Castle Street.
Tel: Conwy 2246
Open daily, April-September, 10am-5.30pm.
Exhibition of Conwy history

Plas Mawr, Conwy
High Street. Fine 16th-century house now home of Royal Cambrian Academy of Art

Smallest House, Conwy
On the quay, open daily during summer

Bodnant Gardens (National Trust), Tal-y-Cafn, Colwyn Bay
Off A470, 5 miles south of Conwy
Beautiful gardens, some of the best in Europe.
Open daily, March-October, 10am-5pm

Gwydir Castle, Llanrwst
Off B5106 close to Llanrwst
Open daily in summer except Saturdays
Historic Tudor mansion with peacocks

Ty Mawr (National Trust), Wybrnant, Gwybernant
3½ miles south west of Betws-y-Coed
Open April-October daily except Saturday, 12pm-5pm.
Birth place of Bishop Morgan. Nature trail

Penrhyn Castle (National Trust), Bangor
A5 one mile east of Bangor
Open every day 1 April-31 October
April, May and October 2-5pm
June-September 11am-5pm
Tel: Bangor 53084
Magnificent Neo-Norman Hall, Railway Museum and Doll Museum. Restaurant

Bryn Bras Castle, Llanrug, Caernarfon
A4086 between Caernarfon and Llanberis
Open Sunday and weekday afternoons May-September, late July and August 10.30am-5pm
Romanesque Castle in extensive grounds

Portmeirion, Porthmadog
Near Minnfordd 2 miles east of Porthmadog
Open daily Easter-October
Italianate village in fine setting and gardens

Plas Newydd (National Trust)
Llanfair, Anglesey
1 mile south west of Llanfair on A4080
Open daily mid April-31 October
Daily except Saturday, 12-5pm
Tel: Llanfair 714795
On edge of Menai Straits, home of Marquess of Anglesey
Military Museum, restaurant

Hafodty Gardens, Betws-Garmon, Caernarfon
4 miles south of Caernarfon on A487
Open daily, no charge but charity collection box

MUSEUMS AND ART GALLERIES

Some museums are run by the local councils and are open all year round. Privately owned ones are generally open only during summer months

Maelor Arts Centre, Rhosddu Road, Wrexham
Tel: Wrexham 2351
Visiting exhibitions and displays

Geological Museum of Wales, Bwlch-gwyn, Wrexham
Adjacent to A525 ½ mile west of Bwlch-gwyn

Daniel Owen Centre Earl Road, Mold
Tel: Mold 4791
Art gallery as well as memorabilia of Welsh author

Canal Exhibition Centre, Llangollen
Close to main bridge over River Dee
Open Easter-end of September
Illustrating events of canal life and history

Grange Cavern Military Museum, Holywell
Off A55 at Holway, near Holywell
Open summer, 9am-6pm, winter 9am-5pm
Collection of military vehicles and militaria in limestone caverns

Rapallo House Museum and Art Gallery
Ffern Road, Llandudno
Open April-November, Monday-Friday
Collection of paintings, sculptures, armour and weapons

Llandudno Doll Museum
Masonic Street, Llandudno
Open Easter-end of September, Monday-Saturday
Collection of old dolls and toy railways

Encounter, North Wales Museum of Wildlife
School Bank Road, Llanrwst
Open Summer: Monday-Saturday, 9.30am-6.30pm
Winter: Monday-Friday, 10.30am-6.30pm
Collection of big game trophies and rare birds both local and from around the world.

Museum of Welsh Antiquities
Fford Gwynedd, Bangor
Visiting exhibitions of painting and sculpture

David Windsor Gallery
High Street, Bangor
Closed Wednesdays, Saturdays and Bank Holidays
Displays of paintings and porcelain from all over the world

Welsh Slate Museum
Llanberis
Tel: 028 682 630
Open daily Easter, 9.30am-5.30pm, May-September, 9.30am-6.30pm
Shows how the slate was won, with orignal machinery and buildings

The Royal Cambrian Academy of Art
Plas Mawr, Conwy
Annual Summer Exhibitions of Welsh Artists

Lloyd George Museum
Llanystumdwy, Nr Criccieth
Open 10am-5pm weekdays May-September
Momentoes of this great man

Segontium Roman fort and Museum
(National Trust)
1 mile south of Caernarfon on A4085
Open mid-March-mid-October, Monday-Saturday, 9.30am-6.30pm, Sunday, 2-6.30pm. Mid-October-mid-March, Monday-Saturday, 9.30am-4pm, Sunday, 2-4pm
Archaeological finds and foundations

Museum of Childhood
Water Street, Menai Bridge, Anglesey
Tel: 0248 712498
Open Monday-Saturday, Easter-October, Monday-Saturday, 10am-6pm, Sunday, 1-5pm
Collection of everying to do with children over the last 150 years

Mostyn Art Gallery
12 Vaughan Street, Llandudno
Open April-September, 11am-6pm, October-March, 11am-5pm
Wide range of contemporary arts from Wales and abroad

Museum of Old Welsh Country Life
Felin Faesog, Tai'n Lon,
Clynnog fawr
East of A499, 10 miles south of Caernarfon
Open April-October, daily 10am-5pm
Folk museum in old corn mill

Almost every village in North Wales has a church of interest. The list is by necessity limited to the major religious sites

Valle Crucis Abbey
Llangollen. 1½ miles out on the A542
Beautiful remains of Cistercian Abbey. Nearby is Eliseg's Pillar

Basingwerk Abbey
1 mile north east of Holywell close to A548
Ruins of monastery founded and famous in 1131

St Winifred's Well
Holywell
Holy well and chapel, place of pilgrimage

St Asaph Cathedral
On A525 6 miles south of Rhyl
Said to be the smallest in Britain, has a collection of old religious papers

Bangor Cathedral
Oldest in continuous use in Britain
In town centre

Penmon Priory
Close to Beaumaris, Anglesey
12th-century remains with holy well and more recent dovecote

Cymer Abbey
Dollgellau
Cistercian monastery in beautiful setting

OTHER ARCHAEOLOGICAL SITES OF INTEREST

Throughout North Wales there are many sites that may be of interest to visitors: Iron Age hillforts, burial sites etc. There are generally marked on Ordnance Survey Maps and make interesting short or long excursions. some of the more important sites are:

Clwyd

Whitford, near Holywell
Wheel cross of 10th-11th century origin. Tallest of its kind in Britain

Eliseg's Pillar, Llangollen
1,000-year-old pillar with long inscription, in field near Valle Crucis Abbey

Offa's Dyke
Crosses country from Llangollen to Prestatyn. Earthwork and bank

Gwynedd

Capel Garmon Burial Chamber, close to Betws-y-Coed
Fine example of neolithic chambered cairn

Tre'r Ceiri, near Nefyn
Superb remains of iron age hillfort on top of The Rivals. Over 200 huts more than 2,000-3,000 years old

Muriau'r Gwyddelod, near Harlech
'Irishmans Walls', remains of circles and enclosures possibly of settlers from across the sea

Roman Steps, near Llanbedr
Line of steps going up and over the valley, unlikely to be Roman

Tomen-y-Mur, near Transfynydd
Roman castle mound and amphitheatre in fine setting

Anglesey

Bryn-Celli-Ddu, near Llanfair
Well preserved mound and chamber from about 2,000BC

Din Lligwy, near Moelfre
Fortified village of variously shaped huts, well preserved in fine setting with several other antiquities close by.

Holyhead Mountain Hut Circles
Close to South Stack. A few huts remaining of large settlement occupied, probably during Roman times around the 3rd century

Caer Gybi, Holyhead
Roman fort almost intact with high walls and towers. St Gybi's church built inside at a later date

---

OTHER PLACES OF INTEREST TO VISIT

Mines

Llechwedd Slate Caverns
Blaenau Ffestiniog
Open daily March-October, 10am-6pm
See a quarry as it was 100 years ago and visit the deepest caverns

Glodfa Ganol Slate Mine
Blaenau Festiniog
Open daily Easter-October, 10am-5.30pm
Machinery and mill in world's largest slate mine. Walk around the caverns

Chwarel Hen
Llanfair, near Harlech
Open Easter-October
Small but old mine, walk in with helmet and light

Power Stations

Ffestiniog Power Station
Tel: Blaenau Ffestiniog 465
Open Easter-October
Pumped storage scheme with low and high reservoirs

Trawsfynydd Power Station
Tel: Trawsfynydd 331
Parties only allowed to visit nuclear power station set amidst mountains

Dinorwic Power Station
Tel: Llanberis 363
Hydro-electical pumped storage scheme built inside a mountain. Information centre only open at present, Easter-September

Wylfa Power Station
Cemaes Bay, Anglesey
Tel: Cemaes Bay 710471
Tours at 10.15am and 2pm Monday-Friday, June-September
Observation tower open daily
Nuclear power station set on rugged coast

Zoos

Welsh Mountain Zoo and Botanical Gardens
Off Kings Road south of Colwyn Bay town centre.
Tel: 0492 2938
Open summer 9.30am-8pm, winter 10am-4pm
Collection of birds of prey and animals in magnificent setting

Jails etc

Beaumaris Jail
Church Street, Beaumaris, Anglesey
Open Daily 11am-6pm, May-September
Grim but interesting, reminder of prison life in the past

Beaumaris Courthouse
Opposite castle entrance
Open all year
Oldest and most original courthouse still being used in Wales

Fort Belan
Near Dinas Dinlle, Caernarfon
Open daily 10am-5.30pm, May-September
Old fort in fine setting, museums, gift shop and flights over Snowdonia

RAILWAYS

There are several narrow gauge railways in North Wales and two lines operated by British rail that offer exciting scenery

Ffestiniog Railway
Runs from Porthmadog to Blaneau Ffestiniog
Operates every day April-September and thereafter a limited service
Tel: Porthmadog 2384
superb run on most famous narrow gauge steam railway

Snowdon Mountain Railway
Llanberis to Snowdon Summit
Daily service April-October, conditions permitting
Tel: Llanberis 223
Rack and pinion steam railway to highest summit in England and Wales

Llanberis Lake Railway
Runs alongside Llyn Padarn through country park
Daily service April-September
Tel: Llanberis 549

Bala Lake Railway
Llanuwchllyn, Bala
Daily service April-September
Tel: Llanuwchllyn 666
    or Bala 520226
Steam railway alongside lake, with magnificent scenery

Conwy Valley Railway Museum
Betws-y-Coed Station
Open daily 10.30am-5pm
Steam miniature railway and historical rolling stock and railway items

Llandudno Cabin Lift
Open daily Easter-September, weather permitting
Swiss-style trip up the Great Orme

Great Orme Tramway, Llandudno
continuous daily service in summer from town to summit

Llangollen Station
By river in Llangollen. Items of interest including locomotives and rolling stock. Steam days.
Open weekdays and weekends in summer, weekends only in winter

British rail operate regular passenger services along the North Wales coast and Holyhead. Two branch lines are worthy of mention because of the magnificent views and situation of the lines:

Conwy Valley Railway
Conwy to Blaenau Ffestiniog
Regular daily service throughout the year
Superb run along valley and through mountains. Can be joined at any station en route

Cambrian Coast Line
Aberystwyth to Pwllheli
Regular daily service
Follows coast across estuaries with sea and mountain views. Can be joined at any station en route

BUS SERVICES

Sherpa Service
A regular bus service operating around Snowdon during Summer for walkers and visitors. Runs from Caernarfon, Llanrwst or Porthmadog

Crossville Bus Company
The area is well served by regular bus services. Tickets are available for local and national services, with some special offers for one-day touring or seven-days touring. The Gwynedd Dayrider ticket allows you to use Crossville and other independent operated services in the country very cheaply for one day.

For latest information it is wise to telephone the local offices listed below:

Crossville offices in Gwynedd:
Amlwch   830280 (Anglesey)
Bangor   2448
Barmouth   280677
Blaneau Ffestiniog   259
Caernarfon   2556
Llandudno   76201
Llangefni   722104 (Anglesey)
Porthmadog   2046
Pwllheli   2458

Crossville offices in Clwyd:
Colwyn Bay   2330
Corwen   2164
Denbigh   2124
Flint   2276
Llandudno   76201
Llandudno Junction Deganwy 81226
Mold   2823
Prestatyn   3887
Rhyl   4723
Wrexham   51156

VISITOR CENTRES

The main visitor centres are operated by the forestry Commission and the Water Authority. They have picnic sites and nature trails around them and provide information on the surrounding areas

Forestry Centres

Gwydyr Uchaf Visitor Centre
One mile west of Llanrwst on B5106 close to Gwydir Castle
Forest exhibition and slide presentation and publications counter

Maesgwm Visitor Centre
Coed Brenin Forest, 8 miles north of Dolgellau on A470
Exhbition depict life and geology of area and nearby gold mines

Beddgelert Campsite
In forest close to Beddgelert
Camping, picnic spots and trails. Details from shop on site

Bod Petrual Visitor Centre, Clocaenog
7 miles south west of Ruthin on B5105
Picnic sites and exhibition of local forests and ecology

Newborough Warren, Anglesey
Close to Newborough town on A4080 west of A5
Picnic spot and information centre on superb sand dunes and forest. On Llanddwyn Island is a nature centre showing local ecology and life as it was

Water Authority Centres

Llyn Alaw, Anglesey
Between A5 and Amlwch
History of lake surrounding wildlife, picnic spot and fishing

Llyn Brenig, Clwyd
$6\frac{1}{2}$ miles south west of Denbigh
Interpretation centre with archaeological trails, fishing and yachting

Electricity Boards Centres
See 'Other Places of Interest' as most Power Stations have visitor centres and nature trails around them

FISHING

In a country so well endowed with rivers, lakes and the sea there is obviously a wide variety of fishing available. It is necessary though to have the required permits for each stretch of inland water. Each small river, stream, lake, reservoir or canal falls within the boundary of the Welsh Water Authority. You must first obtain a licence from them to fish in these waters, then you must obtain a permit (usually available locally) to fish in the relevant stream or lake. Remember the rights to fish any stretch of water belong to the owner of the adjacent bank.

Welsh Water Authority Offices

Gwynedd River Division
Highfield, Caernarfon, Gwynedd
Tel: (0286) 2247

Dee and Clwyd River Division
Shire Hall, Mold, Clwyd
Tel: (0352) 2121

Some lakes for fishing:
Llyn Trawsfynydd
Llyn Tegid (Bala Lake)
Llyn Alaw, Anglesey
Tan-y-Grisiau Reservoir, Blaenau
   Ffestiniog
Llyn Brenig, near Denbigh

Sea fishing is widespread right around the coast of North Wales, providing many varieties of fish and fishing. There are sands, piers and jetties and even rocks to provide a variation for the sea angler. Boats can be hired at several centres for the more adventurous.

The keen angler will probably already have a copy of the excellent publication by the Welsh Tourist Board. The Wales *Angling Guide* available nationally will tell you all you need to know about the inland and sea fishing available throughout Wales

SWIMMING POOLS

There are public swimming pools at many centres throughout North Wales

Clwyd		*Gwynedd*
Corwen	Mold	Bangor
Colwyn Bay	Prestatyn	Almwch
Connahs	Rhyl	Harlech
Quay		
Denbigh	Ruthin	
Flint	Wrexham	
Holywell	Buckley	

SPORTS CENTRES

Plas Arthur Sports Centre, Llangefni
Tel: Llangefni 722966

Holyhead Sports Centre, Holyhead
Tel: Holyhead 4112

Colwyn Bay Leisure Centre
Tel: Colwyn Bay 33223

Deeside Leisure Centre, Queensferry
Tel: Deeside 812311

TOURIST INFORMATION — GANOLFAN CROESO CYMRU

Many towns in North Wales now have tourist offices either run by the local council or the Regional Tourism Council. They are able to provide up-to-the-minute information on what is going on in the area, local timetables and places to visit, plus leaflets on local nature trails and accomodation. The staff are extremely helpful and anxious to see that you get the maximum benefit from your visit to Wales. Most offices are open throughout the summer and are generally easy to find in the town or village, being well signposted.

There are information centres in the following towns:

Colwyn Bay	Tel: (0492) 56881
Betws-y-Coed	Tel: (06902) 426
Blaneau Ffestiniog	Tel: (076 681) 360
Caernarfon	Tel: (0286) 2232
Conwy	Tel: (049263) 2248
Holyhead	Tel: (0407) 2622
Holywell	Tel: (035288) 899
Llanberis	Tel: (028682) 765
Llandudno	Tel: (0492) 76413
Llangollen	Tel: (0978) 860828
Llanrwst	Tel: (0492) 640604
Menai Bridge	Tel: (0248) 712626
Pentrefoelas	Tel: (06905) 640
Porthmadog	Tel: (0766) 2981
Prestatyn	Tel: (07456) 2484
Rhyl	Tel: (0745) 55068
Wrexham	Tel: (0978) 57845

NATURE TRAILS

There are innumerable nature trails and town trails throughout North Wales. Many are run by local authorities, the Forestry Commission or CEGB (at power stations). Most produce individual leaflets containing details of routes, etc. It is therefore wise to enquire locally for these.

The Welsh Tourist Board publishes a booklet available in most shops and information centres, called appropriateley *Walking*, it covers most nature trails and town trails in the area.

GUIDED WALKS

The Snowdonia National Park operates guided walks from various points within the Park, but as these may vary from time to time contact them directly for up-to-the-minute information by telephone at Penrhyndeudraeth 770 274.

Remember that the Welsh for 'Public Footpath' is 'Llwybr Cyhoeddus'

MILLS AND CRAFTS

Many towns have a craft shop or two in the main street, while tourist attractions also usually have an associated craft shop selling locally made artefacts, so it is not feasible to list them all here. This list has therefore been restricted to places of manufacture that can be visited. there are many artisans working in North Wales who make a variety of products, and the local information office will be able to give the most up-to-date information. Below are listed some of the places to visit.

Potteries

Snowdonia Pottery, Beddgelert
Open daily for most of the year

Cae Dafydd, near Beddgelert
Open daily during summer, also has a wildlife sanctuary

Ffestiniog Pottery, Blaenau Ffestiniog
Open all year

Gwynedd Pottery, Fourcrosses, near Pwllheli
Open all year

Conwy Pottery, Conwy
Open all year

Porthmadog Pottery, Porthmadog
Open all year during weekdays

Tyn Llan Pottery, Penmorfa, near Porthmadog
Open weekdays all year, plus weekends in summer

The Saltings Pottery, Penrhyndeudraeth
Open all year, Monday-Saturday

Pretty Ugly Pottery, Caernarfon
Open all year

Brynsiencyn Pottery, Anglesey
Open all year

Woollen Mills and Knitwear

Holywell Textile Mills, Hollywell
Open all year Monday-Saturdays

Brynkir Woollen Mills, Golan, near Porthmadog
Open all year during working week

Penmachno Woollen Mill, near Betws-y-Coed
Open all year during working hours and weekends in summer

Trefriw Woollen Mills, Llanrwst
Open all year during working week and Saturdays and Sundays in summer

Bodeilio Weaving Centre, near Llangefni, Anglesey
Open daily during summer

Llangollen Weavers, Llangollen
Open all year

Flour Mills

Felin Isaf, Llantsantffraid, Conwy Valley
Open Tuesdays-Saturdays, Sunday 2.30pm-5.00pm, April-October

Other Crafts

Maes Artro, Llanbedr, near Harlech
Open everyday during season and some parts throughout the year. Sells and manufactures a wide range of products

Orissor Craft Centre, Corwen
Open Daily
Manufactures and demonstrates many local crafts

Ruthin Craft Centre, Lon Parcwr, Ruthin
A purpose-built craft complex with 14 different craft workers.

ACCOMMODATION

There is a great range of accommodation available in North Wales, everything from caravans and guest houses to luxury hotels. Many visitors will have booked their stay in advance, but for those who cannot, or are content to tour without prior booking, many Tourist Information Centres offer a bed booking service. This service is designed to give information on type, style and prices of accommodation and recommends the most suitable for your requirements. If you prefer to scout about for your own accommodation the Tourist Information Centres can generally supply a list of hotels, guest houses and other beds available in the locality.

Youth Hostels
Throughout North Wales there is a chain of Youth Hostels. These are ideal for all ages, and are not restricted to young people. They are cheap to stay at and are generally in beautiful situations. The dormitory accommodation is excellent and meals can usually be provided.

There are hostels at:

Clwyd

Chester
Colwyn Bay
Cynwyd
Llangollen
Maeshafn

Gwynedd

Bangor
Bryn Gwynant, Beddgelert
Capel Curig
Ffestiniog
Harlech
Idwal Cottage
Llanbedr
Llanberis
Lledr Valley, Dolwydellan
Betws-y-Coed
Penmaenmawr
Pen-y-Pas near Snowdon
Bala
Rowen
Snowdon Ranger

or for further information contact the
Regional Office:
Merseyside Youth Hostels
40 Hamilton Square
Birkenhead
Merseyside

SOME USEFUL ADDRESSES

British Mountaineering Council,
Crawford House,
Precinct Centre,
Booth Street East,
Manchester MI3 9RZ
Tel: 061 273 5835

British Tourist Authority,
64 St James Street
London SW1
Tel: 01 499 9325

Camping Club of Great Britain and
Ireland
11 Lower Grosvenor Place
London SW1 W 0ey
Tel: 01 828 1012

Caravan Club
East Grinstead House
East Grinstead
Sussex RH19 1UA
Tel: 0342 26944

Cyclists Touring Club
69 Meadrow
Godalming
Surrey
Tel: Godalming 7217

Forestry Commission
Churchill House
Churchill Way
Cardiff SY23 2DA

Holiday Fellowship
142 Great North Way
London NW4 1EG

National Trust
42 Queen Anne's Gate,
London SW1H 9AS
Tel: 01 222 9251

National Trust
North Wales Regional Office
Dinas
Betws-y-Coed
Gwynedd LL24 0HG
Tel: Betws-y-Coed 636

National Mountaineering Centre
Plas-y-Brenin
Capel Curig
Betws-y-Coed
Gwynedd
Tel: Capel Curig 214 280

North Wales Tourism Council
Glan-y-Don Hall
Colwyn Bay
Clwyd
Tel: 0492 56881

Wales Tourist Board
PO Box 151
WDO Cardiff CF5 1X5

Outward Bound Trust
14 Oxford Street
London W1
Tel: 01 637 4951

Rambler's Association
1-5 Wandsworth Road
London SW8 2LJ
Tel: 01 582 6768

Youth Hostels Association
Trevalyan House
St Albans
Herts AL1 2DY
Tel: St Albans 55215

Welsh Water Authority
Cambrian Way
Brecon
Powys

Snowdonia National park
Information Office
Hen Ysgol
Maentwrog
Blaenau Ffestiniog
Gwynedd

Index

Aber, 45
Aberconwy House, 45, 116
Aberdaron, 87-8
Aberffraw, 102
Abergele, 34-5
Aberglaslyn Pass, 60
Abersoch, 86, 88
Afon Alwen, 26
Afon Bach, 46
Afon Cefni, 101, 112
Afon Dwyryd, 68
Afon Machno, 78
Afon Mawddach, 74
Afon Tryweryn, 76
Amlwch, 107
Anglesey, 12-13, 16, 94
Arenig Fach, 76
Arenig Fawr, 76
Arenigs, 65

Bala, 76
Bala Lake, 18
Bala Lake Railway, 77, 120
Bangor, 46-7
Bangor Cathedral, 119
Bardsey Island, 87, 89
Barmouth, 13, 70, 74
Basingwerk Abbey, 32, 119
Beaumaris, 96, 110
Beaumaris Castle, 111-13
Beaumaris Courthouse, 111-13
Beaumaris Jail, 111-13
Beddgelert, 58
Beddgelert Forest, 80
Belgian Promenade, 111, 113
Benllech, 109
Bersham, 18, 20
Berwyns, 25-6
Bethesda, 46, 66
Betws-y-Coed, 13, 57
Black Point, 109
Black Rock Sands, 88
Blaenau Ffestiniog, 13, 66-7

Bodelwyddan, 39, 40
Bodnant Gardens, 37, 39, 116
Bodrhydan Hall, 116
Borrow, George, 20, 25
Borth-y-Gest, 83, 88
Brittania Bridge, 96
Bronaber, 77
Bryn Bras Castle, 117
Bryn-Celli-Ddu, 99, 100, 119
Brynkir Woollen Mill, 80, 83
Bull Bay, 107
Butler, Eleanor, 21

Cadair Bronwen, 25
Cader Idris, 74
Caer Drewyn, 26
Caer Gybi, 103, 120
Caer Leon, 44
Caernarfon, 47-8
Caernarvonshire, 12
Canal Exhibition Centre, 21-2, 117
Capel Curig, 57
Capel Garmon Burial Chamber, 58, 119
Carnedd Dafydd, 56
Carnedd Llywelyn, 56
Carnedd-y-Filiast, 55
Carneddau, 46, 49
Castell Dinas Bran, 21-2
Celtic, 11
Celtic Christianity, 16
Cemaes Bay, 107
Cemlyn Bay, 105, 107
Cheshire, 18
Chester, 30
Church Bay, 107
Climbers, 13
Clwyd County Council, 31
Clwydian Range, 18, 27
Clwydian, River, 33
Clynnog Fawr, 92
Cnicht, 60
Cob, The, 81

Coed-y-Brenin Forest, 73-4
Colwyn Bay, 34, 36
Conwy, 42
Conwy Castle, 42, 45
Conwy Falls, 75
Conwy Mountain, 44-5
Conwy, River, 29, 42, 45
Conwy Valley Railway Museum, 57-8, 120
Copper, 13
Corwen, 16, 26-7
Craig Lwyd Axe Factory, 45
Criccieth, 83
Crimea Pass, 67, 75
Croesor, 60
Cwm Bychan, 71
Cwm Nantcol, 71
Cwm Pennant, 83
Cwm Ystradllyn, 83
Cymer Abbey, 119
Cynwyd, 26

Daniel Owen Centre, 30, 117
Dee, River, 18, 20, 23, 27, 30
Deeside, 12
Deganwy, 38
Deiniol Library, 30
Denbigh, 40
Denbighshire, 11, 12
Devils Kitchen, 54
Din Lligwy, 109, 119
Dinas Dinlle, 92-3
Dinorwic Pump Storage Scheme, 54
Dolbadarn Castle, 52
Dolbenmaen, 83
Dolgellau, 74
Doll Museum, Llandudno, 117
Dolwyddelan, 75
Druids, 11, 94, 100, 103
Drum, 56
Dyffryn Ardudwy, 73

Edern, 91
Eglwyseg Mountains, 18, 21-2, 26
Eisteddfod, 11
Eisteddfod, International Musical, 20
Elidir Fawr, 54
Eliseg's Pillar, 22, 25
Ellen's Tower, 103, 105

Erdigg, 19, 20, 116
Ewloe Castle, 30, 33
Exmewe Hall, 27

Fairy Glen, 75
Feilw Standing Stones, 105
Ffestiniog, 13, 67
Ffestiniog Power Station, 69
Ffestiniog Railway, 67, 80, 82, 121
Flint, 11, 18, 30, 33
Flintshire, 29
Foel Fras, 56
Foel Grach, 56
Forest Trails, 13, 17
Fort Belan, 92-3
Fynnon Lloer, 56

Gelert, 58
Geological Museum of North Wales, 20, 117
Gladstone Museum, 30
Gladstone, William, 30
Glantraeth Zoo Gardens, 101
Glodfa Ganol 67, 69, 120
Glyder Fach, 55
Glyder Fawr, 55
Glyders, 49, 54
Gold Mining, 13
Gorphwysfa Hotel, 53
Grange Cavern Military Museum, 32, 117
Great Orme, 35-8
Great Orme Tramway, 121
Gwrych Castle, 34-5, 116
Gwydir Castle, 39, 116
Gwydyr Forest, 39, 56

Hafodty Gardens, 117
Halkyn Mountain, 18, 31
Harlech, 70
Harlech Castle, 71
Harlequin Puppet Theatre, 34
Hawarden, 30, 33
Holy Island, 104
Holyhead, 103-4
Holyhead Mountain, 103, 105, 120
Holywell, 31
Horseshoe Falls, 22-3
Horseshoe Pass, 22-3, 26

Idwal Slabs, 34
Inigo Jones, 39
Iron Ore, 18

Jubilee Tower, 31

King Arthur, 52

Lavan Sands, 10, 96
Lead, 13, 31
Leicester's Church, 39, 40
Lewis Carroll, 38
Little Orme, 34-5
Loggerheads, 27-31
Llanabo, 108
Llanarmon Dyffryn Ceiriog, 25
Llanarmon Glyn Ceiriog, 25
Llanbadrig, 107
Llanbedr, 71
Llanbedrog, 85, 88
Llanberis, 52, 66
Llanberis Lake Railway, 52, 120
Llandanwg, 72
Llandegai, 46
Llandegla Moor, 27
Llandrillo, 25-6
Llandudno, 13, 35
Llandudno Cabin Lift, 120
Llandudno Junction, 42
Llandwrog, 93
Llandwyn Island, 101
Llanfair, 71, 120
Llanfair PG, 97-8
Llanfrothen, 60
Llangefni, 112
Llangian, 87
Llangollen, 16, 18, 20, 23, 26-7
Llangollen Railway Society, 121
Llangollen, Vale of, 25
Llanhaelhaern, 90
Llanrhaedr ym Mochnant, 25
Llanrwst, 39
Llantysilio Mountains, 26
Llanuwchllyn, 77
Llanystumdwy, 85
Llechwedd Slate Caverns, 67, 69, 120
Lledr Valley, 57, 65
Lleyn Peninsula, 81
Lloyd George, 85, 118

Llyn Alaw, 107-8
Llyn Brennig, 39, 40
Llyn Celyn, 76
Llyn Conwy, 75
Llyn Cowlyd, 56
Llyn Crafnant, 56
Llyn Cwellyn, 79
Llyn Cwmorthin, 67
Llyn Dinas, 58
Llyn Eigiau, 56
Llyn Geirionydd, 56
Llyn Idwal, 54
Llyn Mair, 68
Llyn Ogwen, 54
Llyn Padarn, 54
Llyn Peris, 54
Llyn Tegid, 65
Llyn y Cwn, 54
Llyn y Dywarchen, 79

Maddocks, William, 81
Madog of Gruffyd, 23
Maelor Library, 20
Maelor Saesneg, 20
Maen Huail, 27
Maenen, 42
Maentwrog, 68
Maes Artro, 72
Maeshafn, 18
Malltraeth, 101
Marchlyn Mawr, 54
Maritime Museum, 82
Marquess of Anglesey, 97
Mawdach Estuary, 65
Meliden, 32
Menai Bridge, 111
Menai Straits, 46-7, 96
Minera, 18, 23
Minfford, 69
Moel Famau, 31
Moel Fferna, 25
Moel Hebog, 80, 83
Moel Siabod, 57
Moel y Gest, 83
Moelfre, 109
Moelwyn Bach, 60
Moelwyn Mawr, 60
Mold, 27, 30
Morfa Nefyn, 89, 91

Morgan, Bishop, 25
Mostyn Art Gallery, 118
Muriaur Gwyddelod, 70-1, 119
Museum of Childhood, 111, 113, 118
Museum of Welsh Antiquities, 118
Museum of Wildlife, 39, 118
Mynydd Drws-y-Coed, 80
Mynydd Mawr, 79
Mynydd Rhiw, 87
Mynydd y Garn, 105

Nant Ffrancon, 49
Nant Gwynant, 58
Nant Gwrtheyrn, 91-2
Nantlle, 79
Nantmor, 60
Narrow Gauge Railways, 13
National Mountaineering Centre, 58
Nefyn, 89, 91
Newborough, 100
Newborough Warren, 101
North Wales Quarrying Museum, 52, 54, 118

Offa's Dyke, 26, 119
Offa's Dyke Path, 33
Ogwen, 54
Orrissor Craft Centre, 27
Owain Glyndwr, 70, 110
Owen, Daniel, 30-1

Packhorse Road, 54
Padarn Country Park, 52
Parys Mountain, 107-8
Penarth Fawr, 85
Penmachno, 75
Penmaen Rhos, 34
Penmaenmawr, 45
Penmon Head, 109
Penmon Priory, 109, 113, 119
Penrhyn Castle, 46-7
Penrhyndeudraeth, 68
Pensarn, 34
Pentrefoelas, 75
Pen-y-Gwryd, 53
Pen-y-Pas, 53
Pen-yr-Oleu Wen, 56
Pistyll Cain, 73-4

Pistyll Rhaiadr, 25
Plas Brodanw, 60
Plas Goch, 97, 99
Plas Mawr, 43, 45, 116
Plas Newydd (Anglesey), 97, 99, 117
Plas Newydd (Llangollen), 21-2
Plas Tan-y-Bwlch, 67-8
Plas-y-Brenin, 58
Point of Ayr, 32
Ponsonby, Sarah, 21
Pont Cysyllte, 22-30
Porth Colmon, 89
Porth Dinllaen, 90
Porth Iago, 91
Porth Niegwl, 87-8
Porth Oer, 89, 91
Porthmadog, 60, 81
Portmerion, 60, 62, 117
Powys, 25
Prestatyn, 18, 26-7, 32
Puffin Island, 109-10, 113
Pwllheli, 85

Queensferry, 18, 29

Rapallo House, 36, 117
Red Wharf Bay, 109
Rhaeadr Mawddach, 73-4
Rhinog Range, 13, 65, 69
Rhoscolyn, 104-5
Rhosneigr, 101.2
Rhos-on-Sea, 34
Rhosydd Slate Mines, 67
Rhuddlan Castle, 39, 40
Rhyd-Ddu, 75
Rhyl, 33
Richard II, 30
RNLI Maritime Museum, Barmouth, 73
Roman Bridge, 75
Roman Steps, 72, 119
Romans, 11, 13, 18
Royal Cambrian Academy of Art, 43, 118
Royal Welch Fusiliers, 48
Ruabon, 18
Ruthin, 27
Ruthin Castle, 27

Scott, Sir Walter, 21
Segontium, 48, 118
Shell Island, 72
Shropshire Union Canal, 21, 23
Silurian Rocks, 18
Silver Bay, 105
Skerries, The, 105
Snowdon, 13. 49
Snowdon Mountain Railway, 52, 121
Snowdon Ranger Youth Hostel, 79
Snowdonia, 13, 16, 17
Snowdonia National Park, 13, 49
South Stack Lighthouse, 103, 105
St Asaph Cathedral, 39, 40, 119
St Bueno, 92, 102
St Cwyfan, 102
St Cybi, 103
St Giles, 19, 20
St Gwenfaen, 104
St Mungo, 40
St Patrick, 107
St Seriols Well, 109, 113
St Tudwals Islands, 86,
St Winifreds Well, 31, 119
Stanley, H. M., 40
Sun Centre, 33
Swallow Falls, 58
Sychnant Pass, 44-8

Tanygrisiau, 67
Tegfryn Art Gallery, 111, 113
Telford, 23, 25, 42, 46, 96
Theatr Clwyd, 30-1
Theatr Gwynedd, 46-7
Tomen-y-Mur, 75, 119
Traeth Dulas, 108-9
Traeth Lligwy, 108-9

Traeth Mawr, 67, 81
Trearddur Bay, 104-5
Trawsfynydd, 74, 77
Trefriw Woollen Mills, 39
Tremadog, 81
Tremadog Rocks, 82
Tudweiliog, 91
Ty Mawr, 117

University College of North Wales,
46

Vale of Clwyd, 27
Vale of Ffestiniog, 67, 75
Valle Crucis Abbey, 22-3, 26
Valley, 101-2
Vikings, 11

Weavers Loft, 73
Wellington, 21
Welsh Highland Railway, 59
Welsh Mountain Zoo, 35, 120
Whistling Sands, 89, 91
Williams-Ellis, Sir Clough, 68, 85
Wordsworth, 21
Wrexham, 12-13, 18
Wrexham Maelor, 20
Wylfa Power Station, 120

Y Garn, 55
Yale, Elihu, 19
Yale University, 19
Yorke, Simon, 19
Yr Eifl, 90
Yr Wyddfa, 52
Yspytty Ifan, 75

Waterloo Bridge, Betws-y-Coed

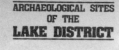

Some Countryside Books from MOORLAND PUBLISHING